BLUE HEELER BIBLE AND BLUE HEELERS

Your Perfect Blue Heeler Guide

Blue Heeler Dogs, Blue Heeler Puppies, Blue Heeler Training, Blue Heeler Grooming, Blue Heeler Health & Care, Blue Heeler Breeders, History, & More!

Mark Manfield

© DYM Worldwide Publishers, 2019.

I0081598

Published by DYM Worldwide Publishers 2019.

ISBN: 978-1-911355-94-6

Copyright © DYM Worldwide Publishers, 2019
2 Lansdowne Row, Number 240 London W1J 6HL

ALL RIGHTS RESERVED. This book contains material protected under International & Federal Copyright Laws & Treaties. Any unauthorized reprint or use of this material is strictly prohibited. No part of this book may be reproduced or transmitted in any form or by any means, electronic, mechanical, or otherwise, including photocopying or recording, or by any information storage or retrieval system without express written permission from the author.

Copyright and Trademarks. This publication is Copyright 2019 by DYM Worldwide Publishers. All products, publications, software, and services mentioned and recommended in this publication are protected by trademarks. In such instance, all trademarks & copyright belonging to the respective owners.

All rights reserved. No part of this book may be reproduced or transferred in any form or by any means, graphic, electronic, or mechanical, including but not limited to photocopying, recording, taping, scanning, or by any information storage retrieval system, without the written permission of the author. Pictures used in this book are royalty free pictures purchased from stock photo websites with full rights for use within this work.

Disclaimer and Legal Notice. This product is not legal or medical advice and should not be interpreted in that manner. You need to do your own due diligence to determine if the content of this product is right for you. The author, publisher, distributors, and or/affiliates of this product are not liable for any damages or losses associated with the content in this product. While every attempt has been made to verify the information shared in this publication, neither the author, publisher, distributors, and/or affiliates assume any responsibility for errors, omissions, or contrary interpretation of the subject matter herein. Any perceived slights to any specific person(s) or organization(s) are purely unintentional. We have no control over the nature, content, and availability of the websites listed in this book.

The inclusion of any website links does not necessarily imply a recommendation or endorse the views expressed within them. DYM Worldwide Publishers takes no responsibility for, and will not be liable for, the websites being temporarily or being removed from the Internet. The accuracy and completeness of the information provided herein, and opinions stated herein are not guaranteed or warranted to produce any particular results, and the advice or strategies, contained herein may not be suitable for every individual. The author, publisher, distributors, and/or affiliates shall not be liable for any loss incurred as a consequence of the use and application, directly or indirectly of any information presented in this work. This publication is designed to provide information regarding the subject matter covered. The information included in this book has been compiled to give an overview of the topics covered. The information contained in this book has been compiled to provide an overview of the subject. It is not intended as medical advice and should not be construed as such. For a firm diagnosis of any medical conditions, you should consult a doctor or veterinarian (as related to animal health). The writer, publisher, distributors, and/or affiliates of this work are not responsible for any damages or negative consequences following any of the treatments or methods highlighted in this book.

Website links are for informational purposes only and should not be seen as a personal endorsement; the same applies to any products or services mentioned in this work. The reader should also be aware that although the web links included were correct at the time of writing they may become out of date in the future. Any pricing or currency exchange rate information was accurate at the time of writing but may become out of date in the future. The Author, Publisher, distributors, and/or affiliates assume no responsibility for pricing and currency exchange rates mentioned within this work.

Table of Contents

CHAPTER 1

Introducing the Blue Heeler

The Blue Heeler may not be a dog breed that appears frequently on lists of the most popular dog breeds, but that just means this breed of dog is a well-kept secret. People who take a Blue Heeler as a pet can attest to the loyalty and friendliness of this breed. Blue Heeler dogs may have been developed to work on farms as herding dogs, but they quickly moved from pastures, to living rooms, where they can be found curled at the feet of their favorite humans today.

Blue Heelers, also called Australian Cattle Dogs, are handsome medium-sized dogs with bright, intelligent, and inquisitive eyes. But it is often the uniquely beautiful coat of the Blue Heeler that attracts people to them. As their name implies, the coat of this dog is bluish gray in color with speckles of brown, black, and white. The perky, over-sized, upright ears give the dog an alert appearance. It's not just for looks, though. Blue Heelers are excellent and dedicated working dogs that are also tuned in to their surroundings. Nothing gets past the ever-vigil Blue Heeler.

The Blue Heeler is an alert and intelligent dog, who perceives its environment very well!

Blue Heelers are quick, athletic animals that love to be active. They can keep up with the activity and bustle of busy families. If you are looking for a companion for your runs, hikes, or outdoor adventures, look no further than the Blue Heeler. The breed has the stamina to join you on your jobs and hikes. In fact, he will thrive on this activity…and provide you with some good motivation to stay active yourself. At about 40 to 45 pounds (18.14 to 20.41 kg), the Blue Heeler is an ideal size for a companion…not too big and not too small.

Blue Heelers really enjoy people. A highly social breed, the Blue Heeler will bond with its owner. The Blue Heeler is a natural born leader, so owners need to socialize the puppies from an early age to firmly establish themselves as the alpha, so the dog doesn't think he is in charge. Therefore, the Blue Heeler will thrive with an owner who is devoted to training the pup and has the time, energy, and experience to set the rules and consistently enforce them. The Blue Heeler dog will be happier when the pecking order is clearly established.

The Blue Heeler guide book is designed to provide you with the information you need to determine if the Blue Heeler is the right dog for you, your family, and your lifestyle. After all, you are adding a new member to your family.

This book focuses on including breed-specific information about the Blue Heeler dog. You will learn about the feeding and nutritional requirements of the Blue Heeler, tips for training your new dog, what to look for when researching Blue Heeler breeders, and ways to keep your pup healthy and active well into his golden years.

Along the way, you will gain a unique insight into this intelligent and hard-working breed and you will appreciate the qualities and attributes of the Blue Heeler. You will quickly learn that Blue Heelers may have a bit of wild Dingo still in them, but they are man's best friend and a loyal and loving companion.

CHAPTER 2

Blue Heeler History

C lues to where and why the Blue Heeler dog was developed can be found in the alternative names of the breed…the Australian Cattle Dog, Australian Heelers, Cattle Dog, and Queensland Heeler. From these, it is clear to see that the Blue Heeler was developed in Australia as a cattle-herding working dog. But the history of the Blue Heeler is a bit more complicated than that. In fact, Blue Heeler history is a subject that is up for much debate.

When Was the Blue Heeler Developed?

The roots of the Blue Heeler dog breed go back almost as far as back as the first European settlers in Australia. The British established the first penal colony in Australia in 1788. Over the next several decades, scientists, naturalists, biologists, and botanists from England and across Europe descended upon the Australian continent to study the strange and diverse wildlife, geology, plant life, and the Aboriginal people. Soon after, colonization of Australia began in earnest.

What Were Blue Heelers Bred For?

The Australian Outback, settlers quickly realized, was prime real estate for cattle ranching. When the ranchers arrived from Europe, they brought with them their trusty herding dogs. While these dogs were excellent herding dogs in England, in the heat and rough terrain of Australia, they faltered. These dogs were simply not suited to the climate and conditions in their new home. It was obvious that a new breed of dog was needed, one with exceptional herding ability, tremendous endurance, but without the heavy coat of the European dogs. Ranchers needed a dog with these traits that they could breed with their own. They found just what they needed right outside their doors.

You can see remnants of its ancestor the Dingo, within the Blue Heeler.

The Blue Heeler's Dingo Connection

The Dingo, the wild dog of Australia, is a medium-sized dog with a sleek, agile body and upright ears. Dingoes are descended from a common domesticated ancestor, the New Guinea Singing Dog, but live a feral lifestyle in Australia. When ranchers began settling Australia, they found that some Dingoes lived in the wild, while some were companions of the Aboriginal people.

The Dingoes were accustomed to the brutal heat and rugged, brushy landscape. They could travel long distances without tiring. They were intelligent, quick, and strong. Ranchers admired these qualities, and sought to breed their own herding dogs with the Australian Dingo.

Hall's Heelers...the Forerunner of Blue Heelers

A European rancher named Thomas Hall is credited with first developing the Australian Cattle Dog, or Blue Heeler breed. Hall's father owned two large cattle stations in New South Wales in the early 1800s and needed work dogs that could handle the terrain and environment. Hall spent a number of years cross-breeding sheepdogs with the native Dingoes of Australia. The wild dogs were known to be timid and leery of humans, so Hall trapped Dingo puppies that were young enough for him to tame. He hand-raised the pups and, when they reached maturity, he bred them with his father's sheepdogs. The resulting pups became known as Hall's Heelers. By 1840, Hall's Heelers were the go-to working dog for Australian cattle ranches.

George Elliot and the Queensland Cattle Dogs

Thomas Hall wasn't the only dog breeder who was working to develop the ideal herding dog for Australian cattle ranches. George Elliot, working on his ranch in Queensland, also felt that mixing the native Dingo with European herding dogs would give him the results he wanted. Several decades after Hall's Heelers became well-established, Elliot was touting the endurance and work ethic of his part-Dingo ranch dogs, often called the Queensland Cattle Dogs.

Blue Heelers inherited the endurance of sometimes harsh natural conditions, from their ancestors.

Robert Kalesky Championed the Blue Heeler.

Blue Heelers owe much to Robert Kalesky. It was through his efforts that the Blue Heeler breed really came into its own. Kalesky, the son of a Polish mining engineer father and an English mother, was born in 1877 in New South Wales. While in his early twenties, Kalesky turned his back on his flourishing law career to immerse himself in the Australian Bush life. As a self-taught naturalist and survivalist, Kalesky was keenly interested in the Blue Heeler dogs. He wrote extensively about the virtues of the dog breed in his popular book, *The Australian Settler's Complete Guide*. This plug helped to introduce a new generation of people to the Blue Heeler.

The Blue Heeler/Australian Cattle Dog Breed is Set

Along the way, two brothers in New South Wales, the Bagust brothers, began breeding Dalmatians with Hall's Heelers. This mix altered the coat colors of the dogs, changing the merle pattern to a speckled pattern. Years later, the American Kennel Club pointed to this mating as the reason for the unique coloring and patterns on the coats of the Blue Heelers.

Australian cattle ranchers continued to employ the Blue Heeler, or Australian Cattle Dog, on their farms and ranches through the 1800s and into the next century. In 1903, the breed standards for the Blue Heeler were officially drawn up.

Hall's Heelers regularly appeared in dog shows in Australia during the 1890s, but their appearances were often limited to shows in New South Wales or Queensland. That all changed with a Blue Heeler dog named Little Logic came on the scene. When

Little Logic was shown in Sydney, he impressed his fans with his appearance, personality, and abilities. Dog lovers clamored for one of Little Logic's offspring. Little Logic, and his best-known son, Logic Returns, were sought-after sires and, by the 1950s, most Blue Heelers could trace their lineage back to these dogs.

Blue Heelers in the United States

Blue Heelers, or Australian Cattle Dogs, as they are also known, were being sent to the United States, Canada, and other areas beginning in the early 1900s. The determined, intelligent, loyal dog was such an asset to cattle ranchers that the demand for the dogs increased. Since the 1930s, however, the American Kennel Club was at a loss as to how to classify the breed. Therefore it fell into a "miscellaneous," catch-all category.

A devoted Blue Heeler owner named Ester Ekman took her dog to a show in 1967 and met Chris Smith-Risk, another Blue heeler owner. The two struck up a conversation and lamented the fact that their dogs were not officially recognized by the American Kennel Club. The pair founded the first breed club, the Australian Cattle Dog Club, in the U.S. Their first order of business was to petition the AKC, for recognition of the breed.

The AKC advised the group to start keeping a record of the dog it registers and to contact breed clubs in Australia for dogs that can trace their parentage back to that country. Over the next decade, the club kept meticulous records and did extensive research on the Blue Heeler breed in general. Finally, in September of 1980, the American Kennel Club fully recognized the breed, which it lists as the Australian Cattle Dog, rather than Blue Heeler. The reason for this is that, depending upon the individual dog's lineage, it could be registered as an American Cattle Dog or an Australian Cattle Dog, to indicate the country that is most prominent in its bloodline.

The Blue Heeler is found throughout the world, and wherever you find him, you'll find him active!

The Blue Heeler in Canada

The Australian Cattle Dogs were recognized by the Canadian Kennel Club about six months before they were added to the American Kennel Club. In Canada, most of the Blue Heelers were working on ranches in the western Provinces but the breed clubs were in contact with each other, and presented an organized front in gathering pedigrees and pushing for official recognition of the breed.

The Blue Heeler in the UK

The Australian Cattle Dog Society of the United Kingdom formed in 1985 and the breed was added to The Kennel Club of the UK almost immediately. Registered Australian Cattle Dogs were first brought to England in the early 1980s, but within a few years, the breed was successfully competing in working trials and obedience classes, proving that the dog from Down Under could hang with the European herding dogs.

Today's Blue Heelers can still be found hard at work on farms and cattle ranches, but more and more of the dogs are companion dogs. All of the traits that make Blue Heeler an excellent worker: dedication, stamina, intelligence, and loyalty, are also the qualities that pet owners love in the dog. The Blue Heeler is not your typical, run-of-the-mill dog. And it is for that reason that this breed is gaining momentum among dog lovers.

CHAPTER 3

Blue Heeler Breed Standards

B lue Heelers are compact, solidly-built, medium-sized dogs that are extremely intelligent and active. Although the Blue Heelers were created by breeding sheepdogs with Dingoes, the wild dogs of Australia, the dogs are wonderful companions and co-workers for humans. They are quick-learners, hard-workers, and loyal friends. The Blue Heelers were developed to enhance these traits, as well as the physical attributes that make them ideal herding dogs for cattle ranches. As the breed spread from cattle ranch to cattle ranch and even into urban areas as pets or dog show participants, the need arose for breed standardization.

What are the Breed Descriptions for the Blue Heeler?

A healthy adult Blue Heeler, or Australian Cattle Dog, will be compact, muscular, and symmetrical. He will have alert, erect ears and wise, curious eyes. The shoulders and necks of the Blue Heelers are powerful and strong, as are the animals' legs and hindquarters. The dog is built for high-level activity and endurance. The short coat keeps the dog from overheating in the hot, unrelenting sun of the Australian outback. The short coat had the added benefit of allowing the Blue Heeler to move easily through the jagged rocks and rough, thorny brush of the Outback without catching its fur and inhibiting its movement.

Blue Heelers usually range from 35 to 50 pounds (15.88 to 22.68 kg), in weight.

How Big Do Blue Heeler Get?

Before you make the decision to get a new dog, you may wonder, "What size are Blue Heelers?" The label of "medium-sized" dog is rather ambiguous. When you consider that some of the smallest dogs, like the Chihuahua, weigh as little as six pounds (2.72 kg) and the largest dogs, like the English Mastiff or the Newfoundland, can weigh up to 200 pounds (90.72 kg), the term "medium" encompasses a big range. Blue Heelers average between 35 and 50 pounds (15.88 to 22.68 kg).

The male Blue Heelers are a bit taller than the females. Males stand as tall as 18 to 20 inches (45.72 to 50.8 cm). Female Blue Heelers, on the other hand, range between 17 and 19 inches (43.18 to 48.26 cm) in height.

What is the Blue Heeler's Personality?

Each individual dog, of course, has its own unique personality, but there were some personality traits that are common to most Blue Heelers. This breed of dog is naturally protective, and has a strong tendency to gravitate toward herding livestock. Both traits that make these dogs perfect for working on cattle ranches.

Blue Heelers have boundless energy. When used as a working dog, the Blue Heeler displays a tremendous amount of stamina and endurance. As a pet, they require lots of daily exercise to keep them fit and healthy. Rigorous exercise also helps to keep the Blue Heeler mentally active. Because he is built for activity, the Blue Heeler gets easily bored, and when he is bored, he can be destructive.

Blue Heelers are extremely loyal dogs, but they can also be strong-willed and suspicious of strangers. They do best with an experienced dog owner who can socialize the pup from an early age, and set firm boundaries and expectations. The dog will know where he stands in the family hierarchy. Once he learns his place, he will be a loyal and loving member of the family.

Not a naturally aggressive breed of dog, the Blue Heeler's protective nature sometimes brings out some aggressive behavior, like nipping and growling. These traits make the Blue Heeler a good watchdog, but owners will need to provide firm guidance to the dog, so that he understands when he should react protectively and when he can stand down.

What is the Blue Heeler's Coat like?

Blue Heelers have a unique double coat with a short, straight, weather-resistant top coat and a fine, dense, undercoat.

All Blue Heeler puppies are born white, solid white, in color. A few weeks after birth, however, they begin to lose their "baby fur" and get the blue or red mottled fur of an adult Australian Cattle Dog. The full adult coat will come in around nine months of age. Owners should regularly brush their puppies going through this transition to loosen and remove the puppy fur, so the adult fur comes in thick and even.

What are the Accepted Coat Colors for Blue Heelers, or Australian Cattle Dogs?

The breed standards of the Blue Heeler, or Australian Cattle Dog, that have been adopted by kennel clubs and breed clubs around the globe recognize five distinctive coat colors for this breed of dog. They are blue, blue-mottled, blue speckled, red-mottled, and red-speckled. The markings of the Blue heeler can be black and tan, red, tan, and black with white.

Very interesting coat color variations are common with Blue Heelers, as in this example.

What Should I Know About Blue-Coated Blue Heelers?

The blue coloring of the Blue Heeler is not exactly blue. It is more of a blackish-gray with a bluish sheen. The American Kennel Club, as well as several other breed clubs for the Australian Cattle Dog, recognizes three types of blue coats for the Blue Heeler. A solid blue, blue mottled, and blue speckled. While they also recognize red mottled and red speckled, they frown upon dogs with a solid red coat.

What Should I Know About Blue Mottled-Coated Blue Heelers?

The Blue Heeler is known for its blue coat. A dog with a mottled blue coat had a base colored coat of bluish-black or silvery-blue, with spots roughly the size of fingertips marking the fur. The dog may have a black mask covering his eyes, or a black patch over just one eye.

What Should I Know About Blue Speckled Coated Blue Heelers?

Blue Heelers often have a blue speckled coat. This refers to small specks of white fur peppering the solid base coat. The more white specks, the lighter the blue color of the coat.

What Should I Know About Red Mottled-Coated Blue Heelers?

Red Heelers have a coat color with a base of red, interspersed with white hairs. It is believed that red-coated Australian Cattle Dogs were created to differentiate them from wild Dingoes. On the cattle ranches of Australia, the Dingoes were predatory pests that would attack wayward animals on the ranches. Therefore ranchers would shoot the Dingoes. The red coat of the domesticated cattle dogs kept them from being mistaken for wild dogs.

A red mottled coat is a coat that has dime-sized spots of color, usually tan, brown, or black, on a background of reddish brown or ginger.

What Should I Know About Red Speckled-Coated Blue Heelers?

The red fur of a Red Heeler may range in color. It could be a light blondish-ginger or a deep, auburn red. A red speckled coat has small white hairs irregularly dotting the fur in a tiny, speckled pattern, like a bird's egg.

With both the red speckled coat and the red mottled coat, the dog may have a solid mask around his eyes or a patch over one of his eyes.

What is a Bentley Star?

One distinguishing feature of the Australian Cattle Dog, or Blue Heeler, is the presence of a marking that is known as the Bentley Star. This is a blaze or splash of white hairs on the forehead of the dog. Although many Blue Heelers have this Bentley Star marking, the absence of a Bentley star is not a reason for disqualification or penalization.

It is possible, as legend says, that dog with a Bentley Star can trace their lineage to one prolific stud dog owed by Tom Bentley. This dominant feature may have been passed down through generations of Blue Heeler dogs.

CHAPTER 4

Is the Blue Heeler the Right Dog For Me?

I f you are looking for a dog to join your active family, a dog who will join you on your daily runs and weekend hiking adventures, or a dog to help out on your farm, the Blue Heeler may be the dog breed for you. If instead you want a dog that is content to lay at your feet all day, that is low-maintenance, or will be crate-bound most of the day, perhaps the Blue Heeler is not the best choice for you. Whenever you decide to bring a new dog into your home, you need to assess your lifestyle and find a dog breed that will fit well into your life. If you don't, you may end up with an unhappy dog that expresses his frustration with negative behavior, such as destructive chewing and barking. No matter how much you like a dog's outward appearance, you need to look closely at breed characteristics and personality traits. If you don't, you are doing a great disservice to the dog.

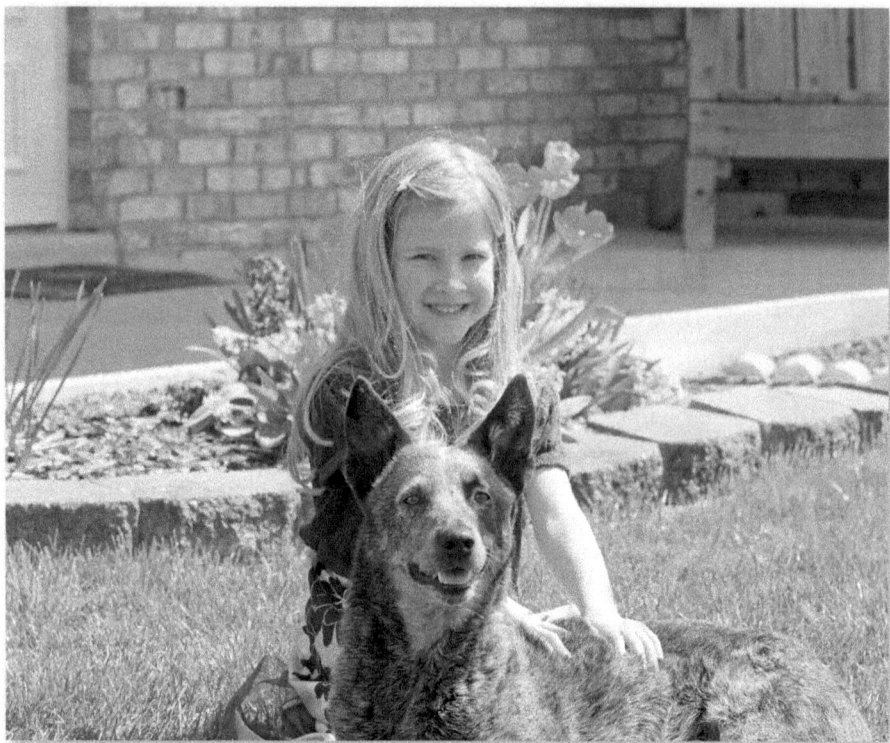

The positive Blue Heeler temperament is one of the best reasons for choosing the breed.

What is the Blue Heeler Temperament?

People often ask, "Are Blue Heelers good pets?" The answer is, yes, Blue Heelers can make wonderful, loyal, and affectionate pets.

Blue Heelers are confident, natural leaders. They have a take-charge attitude. Blue Heelers need to be socialized from an early age, and that socialization needs to be reinforced through their life. Blue Heelers may not be the best breed for first-time pet owners because they need a strong, consistent owner to set boundaries for them and uphold rules.

This doesn't mean Blue Heelers need a mean or aggressive owner. On the contrary, if a Blue Heeler is treated cruelly as a young pup, he will often react by becoming a shy and timid adult dog that is distrustful of people. What is best for the Blue Heeler, or Australian Cattle Dog, is an owner who is firm, but loving.

When raised right, the Blue Heelers become fiercely loyal companions. In fact, many people refer to them as "shadow dogs" because, like your shadow, they are always close by. This closeness can sometimes lead to separation anxiety. If your job requires you to travel frequently or be out of the house for extended periods of time, you may want to reconsider getting a Blue Heeler dog.

In general, however, you can expect your Blue Heeler to be inquisitive, smart, energetic, and loving. He will be devoted to you and your family. Blue Heelers long to stay busy and the dog has boundless stamina. He will relish long walks or runs, socializing with other dogs at the neighborhood dog park, and protecting the farm. If you have some cattle he can herd, he will be all that much happier.

Are Blue Heelers Aggressive Dogs?

Even though Blue Heelers are descended from wild Dingoes, they are typically not aggressive dogs. They are, however, protective of their humans. If they believe their family is threatened or in danger, they will react in an aggressive manner toward the threat. This makes them good, protective watchdogs.

When they are raised in a loving home, however, Blue Heelers respond by being gentle, friendly, and attentive.

What Are the Space Requirements of the Blue Heeler?

Blue Heelers were bred for wide, open spaces. Even today, this breed of dog is better suited for larger living environments, preferably with a large, fenced yard. In fact, the outdoor living space is probably more important than the indoor living space to the Blue Heeler. He will want to spend as much time as possible outdoors.

In the house, the Blue Heeler should not be confined to just one area or one room, but given free range to roam about the whole house. He will want to stay close to his humans, so if his person goes into an upstairs bedroom, the Blue Heeler will naturally want to follow. The dog may experience anxiety if he is not allowed access to the whole house so he can follow his owner everywhere.

Will the Blue Heeler be a Good Addition to My Family?

A Blue Heeler, or Australian Cattle Dog, can be a terrific addition to the right family. Because he needs to stay active and involved, this breed of dog is better suited for young, active families who are on the go. In fact, the Blue Heeler thrives on this sort of energy...as long as he is included in the fun. A Blue Heeler might not be the best choice for a person who is homebound or inactive, a family with very young children, busy working people, or families who travel a lot.

If you want a sporting companion, look no further than the Blue Heeler!

Will a Blue Heeler Get Along with My Children?

Blue Heelers are a good choice for families with children. The dog breed is naturally protective, so it will watch over youngsters. In fact, the Blue Heeler will probably feel like protecting his family is his job…and it kind of is. You may notice, however, that the innate herding instincts of the Blue Heeler comes out when he is playing with children. The dog will want to round the children up and herd them into place!

As with any dog, interaction between a Blue Heeler and small children should always be supervised. You can never be one-hundred percent sure how a dog will react if it is provoked or feels threatened. Also, from an early age, teach children how they should behave around dogs, and how to treat the dogs with love and respect. Teasing and aggravating a dog of any breed may elicit a negative or aggressive response.

Proper socialization ensures that your Blue Heeler can get along with other pets.

Will a Blue Heeler Get Along with My Other Pets?

A Blue Heeler that has been properly socialized from puppyhood is more likely to accept living with other pets. If the animal has not been fully socialized, he may act overly timid or aggressively towards other dogs. When used as a working cattle dog the Blue Heeler is called upon to take charge of the cattle, so Blue Heelers that are pets, will want to do the same thing. If you have another dog or other pets, you should introduce them to your new Blue Heeler slowly, and with supervision. It may take the dogs a few days to figure out where they each belong in the hierarchy, but they should learn to accept their place soon.

Will a Blue Heeler Require a Lot of Exercise?

Blue Heelers, or Australian Cattle Dogs, were developed to work all day on cattle ranches, covering large tracts of land. Today's Blue Heelers still retain all that energy and stamina. They can only burn off that energy with multiple long walks each day. Ideally, the Blue Heeler, or Australian Cattle Dog, should take at least three walks per day, each at least thirty minutes long.

Will a Blue Heeler Require a Lot of Attention?

Blue Heelers are social dogs and thrive on human companionship. They are happiest when they are spending time with their humans, and are known to follow their favorite people from room to room all through the house. Ideally, Blue Heelers should live in a home where at least one person is home with the dog during the day. And even more ideally, that person is active. The perfect situation for a Blue Heeler is to live on a farm or ranch so they have work to keep them busy and long hours outdoors. The Blue Heeler, or Australian Cattle Dog, is not well-suited to spending long hours along or staying cooped up in the house or kennel. This sort of life is no life for the active, intelligent Blue Heeler. He will suffer from depression or act out by barking excessively or being destructive.

What are the Grooming Requirements of the Blue Heeler?

Blue Heelers are a wash and wear dog that doesn't require a lot of grooming and upkeep. The dog breed has a double coat so he should be brushed occasionally to remove the excess fur and any debris that gets tangled in his fur. Blue Heelers do not need to be bathed frequently.

CHAPTER 5

Where Do I Find a Blue Heeler Puppy?

N ow that you have settled on the Blue Heeler as the right dog breed for your new family member, the next step is to find the perfect Blue Heeler puppy for you. Blue Heelers are not as popular as other breeds of dogs, like Golden Retrievers or Labradors, so you may have to do some research to find Blue Heeler breeders in your area. Don't be discouraged if you don't find a Blue Heeler breeder right away. And, don't settle for getting a puppy from a backyard breeder or pet store because you have trouble locating a Blue Heeler breeder. It may take some time, and you may have to travel outside your immediate area, but it will be worth it when you have your top-quality Blue Heeler.

Finding a great quality Blue Heeler may take some time but it's worth it.

Are Blue Heeler Breeders Hard to Find?

When you start your search for a Blue Heeler breeder, remember that this dog breed is also known as the Australian Cattle Dog. In fact, the American Kennel Club lists the breed as the Australian Cattle Dog. You may need to search for both terms to find what you are looking for. Certain regions, states, or areas may have more Blue Heeler breeders than others, especially if they are located in a region where cattle ranches are found.

How Do I Find a Responsible Blue Heeler Breeder?

Don't rely on the internet or newspaper ads to find a reputable Blue Heeler breeder. Ask your veterinarian. Find a Blue Heeler or Australian Cattle Dog breed club. Ask friends or acquaintances who own Blue Heelers. You could even strike up a conversation with a Blue Heeler owner at your neighborhood dog park. You may find that a current Blue Heeler owner is a wealth of information about breeders. It may take a bit of effort, but you should be able to find Blue Heeler puppies for sale near you.

What Should I Ask a Blue Heeler Breeder During a Phone Interview?

When you find a Blue Heeler or Australian Cattle Dog breeder, your first contact with them will probably be via telephone. This is your first opportunity to screen the breeders. Before you make the call, you should write out all of the questions that you can think to ask. If you have your questions written out, you will be sure you won't forget anything when you are deep in conversation with the breeder. Don't worry about asking too many questions. A reputable breeder will not be annoyed or offended by your questions. In fact, they will be happy that you are concerned enough to ask so many questions. It will show them that you are serious about making the right choices. If the breeder does seem to be bothered by your phone interview, this might be a red flag that the breeder is not reputable.

It may be tempting to do all of your communication with the breeder through email or text. But your first interaction with the breeder should be over the telephone. You can gauge a lot more about the breeder from talking to them directly rather than through writing. If the breeder is not willing to talk to you, if he or she is distracted or dismissive over the telephone, or if they are not able to answer your questions, you may view these as red flags.

Some of the questions you should as the Blue Heeler breeder include: "Are the puppy's parents on site?", "How long have you been breeding Blue Heelers?" "Why did you want to breed Blue Heelers?", "Do you breed any other dog breeds?", and "Have the puppies been vaccinated and de-wormed?" If you are dealing with a responsible breeder, they will have no issues answering your questions.

Ask for references. A good reputable breeder should be willing to supply you with the names of people who have purchased dogs from them in the past. Follow up on these. Give that person a quick call to find out if they were happy with their dog-buying process, and if they got a healthy Blue Heeler pup.

What Should I Look For When I Visit a Blue Heeler Breeder's Kennel?

From your phone interview with the Blue Heeler, you should be able to weed out some of the Blue Heeler breeders, so there will be only a few contenders left. At this time, you will want to plan a visit to the breeder's kennel to see the facility and Blue Heeler puppies. At the kennel visit, you should evaluate the facility as best you can, even though you will probably be distracted by the adorable puppies.

When you are at the breeder's kennel, you should take a critical look at the place. Is the kennel clean? Are the puppies kept in a roomy, airy, secure space? Are the dogs housed with other animals, like goats, cows, or chickens? Do the puppies look healthy, socialized, well-fed, and clean? Are the puppies playful and friendly? Or, are the puppies timid and skittish?

You are selecting a companion for your life, be selective!

You should also evaluate the breeder. Is he or she rushing you through the process? Do they seem reluctant to show you certain parts of the kennel? Is the breeder acting like a pushy salesman?

Some less reputable breeders, who are only interested in the sale, know that it will be hard for you to leave the kennel without a cute Blue Heeler puppy in hand. They are counting on your emotions, and the pup's cuteness, to close the deal. But remember that you are the consumer and you don't have to make a purchase if you are hesitant. The puppy buying decision should be made with your head and not your heart. You should mentally prepare yourself to walk away if you are not satisfied with the breeder or the conditions of the breeding facility. In fact, discuss this possibility with everyone who will be accompanying you to the breeder's kennel, so you are all on the same page and no one is disappointed if you end up not buying a puppy that day. If you are buying the Blue Heeler puppy with a spouse or partner, it is okay to ask the breeder to give you a moment alone to discuss it over with your spouse or partner. A good breeder will understand.

Lastly, remember that you probably won't be bringing your new Blue Heeler or Australian Cattle Dog puppy home the same day as you visit the breeder. The puppies should not leave their mother until they are around eight weeks old. They should also be vaccinated, weaned, and socialized. But once you have made your decision and picked out your new puppy, the breeder will have some paperwork to go over with you. One of these will be a breeder's contract which will offer a money-back guarantee about the quality and overall health of the puppy. You will also get copies of the Blue Heeler puppy's medical history, vaccination record, pedigree, purebred registration application, and information on the diet your puppy has been fed.

How Do I Find a Blue Heeler Rescue Organization?

If you are considering rescuing a Blue Heeler, your first question may be "How do I find a Blue Heeler or Australian Cattle Dog rescue organization near me?" There are a number of breed-specific rescue organizations set up around the globe. One of the best ways to find one near you is to search online – on sites like Pet Finder, Adopt A Pet and Petango, but you can also ask your veterinarian, local breeders, and breed clubs if they can point you toward a Blue Heeler rescue group. It is also possible to check with animal shelters in your area. The biggest drawback to adopting a rescue dog is that you don't know the dog's backstory and medical history. However, rescuing an animal can be very rewarding and there are so many wonderful dogs that need new homes.

CHAPTER 6

What Should I Be Cautious of with Blue Heeler Puppy Mills and Backyard Breeders?

When you begin looking for a Blue Heeler puppy, you may not know what you should be looking for in a breeder. There is a big difference between a reputable dealer who is committed to upholding the integrity of the breed, and a puppy mill, or backyard breeder who is only in it for the money. Fortunately, there are good, responsible breeders who produce healthy, genetically sound puppies. Your task is to weed out the backyard breeders and puppy mills and find the Blue Heeler breeders with integrity. What are the differences between Blue Heeler puppy mills, Blue Heeler backyard breeders, and Pet Store puppies?

How Do I Know If I Am Dealing with a Puppy Mill Breeder?

Before you start puppy shopping, you should familiarize yourself with the warning signs that may indicate that you may be dealing with a puppy mill. You should also understand what, exactly, puppy mill breeders are.

A puppy mill breeding operation typically puts profits ahead of the well-being of the puppies. Many of their practices are designed to keep expenses low. For example, a puppy mill may sell puppies that are younger than eight weeks old or may offer unvaccinated pups. In fact, the puppies probably haven't seen a veterinarian at all. Puppy mill breeders most often feed the puppies a less expensive brand of dog food, that is not nutritionally sound. Lastly, puppy mill breeders will breed the females as soon as they can, without allowing them time to recuperate between litters.

Some Blue Heelers are unfortunately bred in less than ideal conditions.

You should never agree to purchase a puppy until you visit the breeder and see the living conditions of the puppies. In many cases, but not all, the puppies in a puppy mill are kept in overcrowded and filthy conditions, and no attempt is made for socializing the new puppies.

Blue Heeler puppies that are bred at puppy mill facilities are more likely to develop genetic issues. Because the puppy mill breeders are focused on making money, they do not necessarily breed dogs for superior quality and breed standards. If a puppy has a physical defect or health issue, that fact is often concealed from the buyer in an attempt to move the product. You may discover later on, that your Blue Heeler puppy from a puppy mill has a genetic or skeletal defects, epilepsy, respiratory problems, or skin disorders.

What Are Some Signs To Look For That May Indicate I Am Contacting a Puppy Mill?

Puppy mills thrive on unsuspecting people who are not experienced in finding reputable Blue Heeler dog breeders. Always be wary when answering an ad online, or in the newspaper, for Blue Heeler puppies for sale. This is especially true if the price is low. Be suspicious if the breeder wants to come to you or meet you at a different location. This may be a sign that they are trying to keep the living conditions of the Blue Heeler puppies hidden from you. If you were dealing with a reputable Blue Heeler breeder, he or she would welcome you to their kennel. Established breeders want to be as transparent as possible. As part of the puppy buying process, they will want you to meet the pup's parents, and observe how he interacts with his brothers and sisters. They want you to see the clean, dry, comfortable living condition at the kennel.

You may encounter a breeder who offers you a discount because the puppies have not been vaccinated. This is also a red flag that you are dealing with a puppy mill. By the time the puppies are ready to leave their mother, when they are at least eight weeks old, they should have had a visit with the veterinarian and gotten their first round of puppy vaccines. If they haven't, it is an indication that the breeder is more concerned about money and expenses, than he or she is about the welfare of their puppies.

You should also ask about the Blue Heeler pup's pedigree. A good, responsible breeder will be able to provide you with documentation showing the animal's lineage and health history going back at least five generations. If the breeder is unable or reluctant to provide this to you, it is a sign that the breeding operation is not concerned about the quality and standards of the puppies, as much as they are about making a profit from them.

Though all Blue Heelers can be charming, don't select one from the wrong place because it encourages further abuse in the industry.

What Should I Know About Pet Store Puppies?

A visit to the local mall often means a stop at the pet store to see the adorable, playful puppies. You should know that the Humane Society of the United States says that 99% of the puppies sold at pet stores come from puppy mills. The employees at the pet stores have been trained to tell you differently or lied to, so they believe that the animals have come from responsible breeders. But the fact remains, that nearly all pet store puppies started life at a puppy mill. The Humane Society routinely investigates pet stores and puppy mills, and reports that many multiple violators of the Federal Animal Welfare Act repeatedly sell their puppies to pet stores. Reputable Blue Heeler dog breeders don't want to sell their puppies through a third party. They want to meet the owners, so they are assured that the dog is going to a good home.

What Should I Know About Backyard Breeders?

Backyard breeders differ from puppy mills, in that breeding and selling puppies is not their sole business. Typically, a backyard breeder is an amateur dog breeder, often totally inexperienced, who thinks his or her Blue Heeler is really great, and attractive, too. They meet someone else with a Blue Heeler and decide that it would great for the dogs to have puppies together. Unlike puppy mills, backyard breeders probably take excellent care of their dogs and are devoted to the breed, but they are inexperienced and lack the knowledge to breed their dogs to meet the standards of the Blue Heeler. They are not abreast of current breeding practices, and do not know how to breed for specific physical or personality traits. They may produce a litter of puppies that are cute, happy, and healthy, but they may not meet breed standards, and they could have underlying genetic problems. As much as you may love your Blue Heeler, it is best to leave dog breeding to the experts.

A Final Word About Puppy Mills, Pet Store, and Backyard Breeders

The only way to put an end to puppy mills and backyard breeders is to stop buying animals from them. This will force them out of business. Purchasing a Blue Heeler puppy is a big decision and one that should be made with the head instead of the heart. Whenever you go to see puppies that you are considering buying, you should be prepared to walk away without a puppy in your arms. Too many people see a cute, little Blue Heeler puppy living in poor conditions at a puppy mill, and think that they are "saving" the dog by buying it. But what they are really doing is supporting a puppy mill and allowing the practice to continue. The entire Blue Heeler dog breed is relying on us to be good stewards of the breed and to make sure that the dogs are genetically sound and healthy, and are bred to the highest standards.

CHAPTER 7

How Do I Prepare to Bring My Blue Heeler Home?

A new puppy will have an easier time adjusting to his new home if his owners are prepared. Before you welcome your new Blue Heeler puppy into your life, you should plan ahead so that you are ready to give your new family member a smooth transition into your home. This doesn't just mean having puppy food and toys on hand. It also means puppy-proofing your home, and preparing your family members and other pets for the new addition. Throughout this chapter, we will take a look at ways that you can prepare your home for your new Blue Heeler puppy.

How Do I Puppy-Proof My Home For My Blue Heeler Puppy?

Most likely, you will pick out your puppy a few weeks before you actually bring him home, so you will have plenty of time to puppy-proof your home. You should take puppy-proofing seriously; although you may think that the puppy-proofing is for your benefit, to protect your belongings from a puppy that likes to chew or isn't house broken. But puppy-proofing is primarily done to keep your new puppy safe. You will need to eliminate anything in your home that may pose a danger to your new Blue Heeler puppy. You also need to take a critical look at your home from your puppy's point of view. That may mean getting down to your puppy's level, on your hands and knees. From this vantage point, you may see hazards that you may have missed, from above.

Remember that your Blue Heeler puppy will be very curious about his new home. To make sure that your home is completely puppy-proof, go carefully from room to room inspecting every corner of the space. Look for electrical cords that your puppy may chew on, small coins or other objects that your puppy may eat, and carpet nails, or other sharp objects that may injure your Blue Heeler puppy.

Remember when puppy-proofing, your Blue Heeler is a lot lower down than you are!

Each room of your house has its own set of unique hazards that could be detrimental to your puppy. In the kitchen, for example, a Blue Heeler puppy may get into the kitchen trash and eat scrap bones, coffee grounds, and other garbage items that might be harmful, even potentially deadly. Your clever Blue Heeler puppy may even be able to open the cabinet door to get to cleaning supplies and detergents. These chemicals are very dangerous to puppies. He may even be able to get into the cupboards where food is stored, and tear open cereal boxes, or bags of dried pasta, or loaves of bread. Child-safety latches installed on your cabinet doors could prevent a deadly accident.

In the bathroom, a curious Blue Heeler puppy could also discover the cleaning supplies that are stored there. And the bathroom trash could also hold dangers, such as ponytail holders, disposable razors, and cotton swabs. Return medication to the medicine cabinet after using it. One of the biggest dangers in the bathroom, however, is the toilet. A thirsty puppy could drink out of the toilet bowl and ingest the cleaning chemicals in the water, which could sicken your dog. Even if you are diligent about keeping his water bowl filled, your puppy could sample the toilet water out of pure curiosity. Encourage everyone in the family to put the lid down after using the toilet. You may need to leave a note in the bathroom to remind them, at least until it becomes a habit.

Even bedrooms are not entirely safe for new puppies. The highly-developed sense of smell that Blue Heelers have means that they are attracted to items that smell like you, their favorite human. The clothes that you leave on your bedroom floor can be too much of a temptation for a little puppy. You may find that shoes, belts, socks, underwear, and other apparel items become favorite chew toys for your new puppy. You could scold the puppy and hope it doesn't happen again, or simply put your dirty laundry in the hamper, so it is out of reach for the pup.

It is not just clothing items that Blue Heeler puppies enjoy chewing. Eyeglasses, hearing aids, and dental retainers are also up for grabs. These items should always be kept out of reach of your puppy. Remember, as your Blue Heeler puppy grows, he will be able to reach places he couldn't before, like your nightstand.

Don't forget the garage when you are puppy-proofing your home. The garage is where people typically store some of the most dangerous products in their homes, such as automotive chemicals, cleaning supplies, pest control chemicals, and lawn and garden fertilizers. All of these can be toxic and may cause death in your Blue Heeler puppy. Chemicals should all be placed on high shelves, or in cabinets with secure doors so that an inquisitive pup can't accidentally get into them.

Throughout the rest of your home, there are other hazards to remove when puppy-proofing your home. Some common houseplants, such as aloe, philodendron, jade plants, and lilies, can be highly toxic to dogs. Curious puppies may nibble on plant leaves and could become very ill if they get ahold of the wrong house plant. Prevention is the best option. All of your houseplants should be discarded, or placed on high, secure areas, well out of reach of active pups. Other household items, such as earbuds, cell phone chargers, TV remote controls, tennis shoes, and beloved stuffed animals may not hurt the puppy too much but could be expensive and upsetting, if the Blue Heeler puppy were to chew them up.

Lastly, you may want to install a baby gate at the top and bottom of the staircase in your home. Young Blue Heeler puppies may not be coordinated enough at first, to negotiate steps successfully and could take a nasty fall. In addition, some studies seem to suggestion that there is a link between early stair use and hip dysplasia later in life. Just to be safe, you may want to prevent your puppy from running up and down the stairs.

How Do I Introduce My Blue Heeler or Australian Cattle Dog Puppy to My Family and Other Pets?

Slowly and calmly is the best answer to this question! The moment you bring your new Blue Heeler or Australian Cattle Dog home is an exciting time for you and your family, but for your new puppy and the other animals in your home, it is a stressful time. You need to make sure that you do all you can, to reduce the anxiety levels of your new puppy, and your current pets.

Blue Heelers can adapt to nearly any situation, with the right encouragement.

Your family members, especially children, may want to gush over the new puppy and hold him tight. As huggable as the cute little Blue Heeler puppy is, he will become anxious and overwhelmed if he is held too much, hugged too much, and passed around from stranger to stranger. Remind your family to refrain from being too attentive and overbearing, with the new puppy. It is okay to put him down and let him explore his new home on his own, under your watchful eye.

Prior to homecoming day, talk to your children about expectations for the new puppy. Let them know that the Blue Heeler puppy is just a baby and that he is probably frightened and nervous. Remind the children that they need to keep the noise level down in the home, no screaming, yelling, or loud music. They also need to do their part to create a calming, chaos-free setting for the new puppy. They need to avoid running from room to room, rough-housing with each other, and agitating behavior. Children should try to act the same way they would if a newborn baby was in the house. If parents discuss this with their children before the puppy comes home, and the children are clear on expectations, the parents should only need to remind an over-excited child about these expectations, on the day of the puppy's welcome home. If parents do not prepare their children before the puppy arrives, they may find that they have to intervene in their child's behavior, and maybe even have to discipline the child. None of this makes for a calm and peaceful homecoming for the pup.

As for preparing your other pets for the arrival of the new Blue Heeler puppy, it may be a bit more difficult. You cannot have a heart-to-heart chat with your dog or cat to let them know what is coming, and how they should behave. But that doesn't mean you can't help to prepare them. If you current pets are not used to being around other animals, you should introduce them to other pets as soon as possible. Visit the neighborhood dog park, go for a walk on a pet-friendly trail, or invite friends with dogs or cats to come over for a playdate. Closely watch how your dog or cat interacts with other animals.

Dogs can be territorial over their homes and owners. Consider introducing your dog to your new Blue Heeler puppy in a neutral location, such as a park or veterinarian's office, so they can get to know each other, without your older dog feeling threatened.

At your home, closely monitor the interaction between your older pets and your new puppy. Even older dogs that have always behaved in a sweet and gentle way, may lash out unexpectedly if they feel like their territory is being threatened. Older dogs and cats may also be less tolerant of a playful, exuberant puppy. If the Blue Heeler puppy jumps and yips, an older dog may snap at him. It is never a bad idea to have a crate or baby gate on hand to separate your pets if you feel it is necessary. But rest assured, in a few days, once the excitement has died down and the pets have gotten accustomed to each other, your animals will begin to build relationships.

What Blue Heeler Supplies Do I Need? Blue Heeler Gear

In the days leading up to your puppy's arrival, you should gather the Blue Heeler supplies that you will need. Having everything on hand is much more convenient than running out to the store in the midst of your puppy's homecoming to buy food, toys, or supplies. This can be disruptive to your pup and cuts into your puppy bonding time. But what Blue Heeler supplies do you need? Here are some suggestions.

This owner was prepared when the puppy came home, a much more peaceful experience.

First, you will need to have a food dish and water bowl for your puppy. There are no breed-specific Blue Heeler food bowls or Blue Heeler water bowl, except for, perhaps, decorative ones. At your local pet store, you will find a wide variety of pet food and water bowls and, honestly, any of them will get the job done. But some may be better than others. Plastic dishes can sometimes be harder to clean than stainless steel ones. Additionally, a playful puppy may chew up a plastic food or water dish! He cannot do this with a stainless steel one. Another option to consider is buying a heavy stone or ceramic dish. Be sure to choose one that is heavy enough, so that your puppy won't accidentally tip it over.

You will also see a dual bowl dish, one unit that has two bowls, one for food and one for water. Some pet owners find these to be very convenient, but others prefer single dishes. It is really a matter of personal preference; your puppy won't care which one you use.

Automatic dog waterers are available that keep your Blue Heeler water bowl continuously filled with fresh water. This is a convenient choice if you find that your dog's bowl is constantly empty. You will also see automatic dog food feeders on the market but be careful using these. It is hard to monitor exactly how much food your dog is eating with an automatic feeder.

Lastly, while you are in the dog food bowl aisle at the pet store, consider buying a couple of collapsible, travel food and water dishes. These are usually made of a flexible plastic and are designed to collapse flat. Most even have a tab with a hole in it, so you can attach it to a backpack using a carabiner (a special shackle with a metal loop). Get at least two, one for food and one for water, so you have a way to feed and water your Blue Heeler puppy when you are away from home, and on the go. This is one Blue Heeler accessory that you will use often.

Along with food and water bowls, you should have puppy food and treats at your house and ready for your Blue Heeler's arrival. Blue Heeler puppies can have sensitive tummies, so you want to pay particular attention to the puppy food that you buy. In fact, it is a good idea to ask the Blue Heeler breeder you are buying your puppy from to tell you the brand of puppy food they have been giving to their pups, so you can get that kind. If you want to switch to a different brand of food, you should do so after your puppy has settled into your home, so you are not overwhelming him with too many changes at once.

Different tap waters have different tastes. Sometimes, dogs will refuse to drink water that tastes different than what they are used to. Consider asking the Blue Heeler breeder for a few jugs of water from their kennel to give your puppy, for the first few days. You can gradually switch him over to your tap water after a few days.

When you purchase puppy food for your new Blue Heeler, you will probably be tempted to buy some treats, too. That's not a bad idea. Treats are a good training incentive for young pups. Just be sure you don't overdo it with too many Blue Healer treats. If he fills up on too many treats, he won't eat his much-healthier puppy food, and he may even develop an upset digestive system.

When purchasing Blue Heeler gear for your new puppy, you will want to buy a collar or harness, and a leash. You should help your Blue Heeler get used to wearing a collar or harness, right away. You never want your dog to go outside without his collar or harness on. After all, these will have tags on them with important contact information, just in case your curious Blue Heeler puppy slips away from you. Remember that your new puppy is just a baby with delicate skin. Choose a Blue Heeler collar that is made of a soft, flexible material, like nylon or leather. A metal collar may be uncomfortable against his skin. Finding the right fit for your Blue Heeler or Australian Cattle Dog collar is very important. You want a collar that fits snugly, but not too snugly. On the other hand, you don't want it to be too loose either. Experts recommend that you adjust the collar so that you can easily place two fingers between it and the dog's neck.

When taking your Blue Heeler or Australian Cattle Dog for walks, you may want to use a harness instead of attaching the leash to his collar. There are a few reasons why a harness is better for your puppy. A harness fits more securely than a collar. Because it goes across the dog's chest, your puppy can't slip out of it, like he could with a collar. A harness is safer for your dog, too. An active Blue Heeler puppy may run and pull on the leash. If he were wearing a collar, he would choke himself. But with a harness, the force is distributed across his back and chest, instead of his neck and throat. As with the collar, be sure to select a harness that is soft and has some give to it, like a nylon or leather one.

As for the leash itself, the clip that latches it to your dog's collar or harness is what is most important. Thoroughly check the clip to make sure it is in good working order. If the moveable part doesn't line up, or the spring doesn't keep it closed, you may find that the leash fails you when you need it most. With leashes, this is the one time when a metal product might be better. A metal Blue Heeler leash is hardier and sturdier. Your dog may nibble on a nylon or leather leash, causing it to snap. But the metal one will hold up. Another option is to consider retractable leashes. Here, the opinions seem mixed. Some people rave about them, and others state that they are prone to breaks.

Your Blue Heeler needs a nice, comfy dog bed. Many dog experts recommend getting a dog crate (kennel) for you puppy. Some dog owners balk at this, but studies have shown that Blue Heelers, and in fact, all dog breeds prefer to have a place of their own, where they feel safe and secure. The crate turns into the dog's sanctuary where he can go to unwind when he feels overwhelmed. You should treat the crate like the doggie palace that it is. Add a padded, comfortable dog bed, preferably one with tall sides. This will add to the enclosed feeling that adds to the sense of security. Make sure the Blue Heeler dog bed you buy is easily washable, so you can regularly clean it.

Young puppies like to chew on things, so consider getting some Blue Heeler dog toys for your new addition. Look for toys that are designed for medium-sized dogs and are made of durable material. Cheaper quality toys may shred or splinter, creating a choking hazard. Remember that your Blue Heeler will appreciate more than just chew toys. He will also like tug o'war toys and fetching toys, like balls and Frisbees. Your Blue Heeler puppy should have access to several different toys so he can have some variety. If your Blue Heeler does not have toys to play with, he just might use some of your belongings as toys!

Blue Heelers really aren't that high maintenance, given their hardiness.

Dogs have existed for thousands of years without cute little sweaters and raincoats, so purchasing these items is one hundred percent optional. But many dog owners look for Blue Heeler dog clothes because they make them happy. You will not need Blue Heeler puppy clothes to have a happy and healthy puppy, but if you see an adorable doggie shirt that you can't resist, it is certainly fine to dress your pup.

Blue Heelers are fairly low-maintenance when it comes to grooming. But you should have some gentle puppy shampoo on hand, in case your puppy takes a tumble in the mud. If you already have the Blue Heeler dog shampoo at your house, you won't have to figure out how to keep your puppy from messing up the house while you run to the pet store. You will be all ready for a puppy bath. As for doggie brushes, it may be a good idea to buy a gentle brush for occasional use, but the short fur of the Blue Heeler doesn't really need a lot of brushing.

CHAPTER 8

What Should I Feed My Blue Heeler?

We all understand that people need to eat healthy, nutritious food, so we avoid conditions like obesity, feel good, and have energy. The same is true with dogs. We all want our dogs to stay in peak health, be active and pain-free, and be happy. The best way to ensure this, is with proper nutrition. Finding the ideal pet food, however, can be a daunting task. There are many options from which to choose. Throughout this chapter, we will look at the feeding and nutritional needs of your Blue Heeler, so you can make informed decisions about your dog's food.

What Are the Nutritional Requirements of Blue Heelers?

The Blue Heeler may be a medium-sized dog, but they are a high-energy breed that was developed for herding. They need a food that can keep up with them. Like all dogs, Blue Heelers need enough protein to build strong muscles. But not all protein is created equal. The bulk of the protein your Blue Heeler, or

Australian Cattle Dog, eats should come from top-quality animal sources, as it is easier for your dog to digest and absorb the nutrients from animal protein. In addition, animal protein contains fat, which is a vital source of energy for Blue Heelers. Lastly, animal protein has ten essential amino acids.

What Should I Feed My Adult Blue Heeler?

As your Blue Heeler matures into adulthood, you will switch from his puppy food to an adult formula dog food. Look for a Blue Heeler adult dog food that contains at least 18% protein and 5% fat. If your Blue Heeler or Australian Cattle Dog is a true working dog that spends long days herding cattle and working on the ranch or is otherwise very active, you may want to feed him a dog food that is higher in protein and fat. The additional protein aids in muscle maintenance, and the added fat provides more energy.

Carbohydrates give your Blue Heeler the fuel he needs to keep him going all day long. When it comes to carbohydrates, the important thing to consider is the digestibility of the carbohydrate. Whole grains, legumes, and vegetables should be fresh and as unprocessed as possible because they will be easier to digest and contain more vitamins and minerals. Look for a brand of dog food that has a crude fiber content of between 3% and 5%.

How Much Should I Feed My Blue Heeler?

How much you feed your dog is always a tricky thing. But consider this: an adult Blue Heeler that weighs between 30 and 50 pounds (13 to 22.6 kg), should consume around 20 or 30 calories per pound of body weight, per day. So, a Blue Heeler that is on the larger side would need to eat roughly 1,500 calories every day. Of course, Blue Heelers that are extremely active should have a higher calorie intake. Remember that this is a per day amount. You will need to divide the total calorie requirements by two or three, depending on how many meals you will be serving your dog each day.

Healthily-fed Blue Heelers have unmistakable energy and playfulness!

What Should I Feed My Blue Heeler Puppy?

Blue Heeler puppies need more protein and nutrients than adult dogs. That's so that the pup can build strong, healthy bones and muscles. Dog food that is formulated for adult Blue Heelers simply does not have enough calories, protein, fat and vitamins for a growing pup. Ideally, a Blue Heeler puppy food should have a minimum of 22% protein, and 8% fat, to help him get a great start in life.

A young Blue Heeler puppy, up until he is about 12 weeks old, should have several smaller meals each day…ideally four meals. Offer your Blue Heeler puppy his food dish, and let him eat for about ten minutes. After ten minutes, remove the food bowl and discard the uneaten portion. But note how much he is eating each time, and increase it as he grows bigger.

At around three months, you can phase out one of the feedings, and go down to just three meals per day. During this time – from three months to about six months of age – your growing Blue Heeler will start to change from a roly-poly puppy, to a sleek, muscular adult dog. He may look like a full-grown Blue Heeler, but he still has the nutritional needs of a puppy. He should still eat his Blue Heeler puppy food, until he reaches his first birthday. After that time, you can switch your dog to an adult Blue Heeler dog food.

What Should I Feed My Senior Blue Heeler?

Blue Heelers enter their senior years when they reach about ten years of age. At this time in their lives, Blue Heelers start to undergo a number of changes. The nutritional needs also change, particularly as the Blue Heeler becomes less active. Of course, he will not need to consume as many calories if he is not burning them. At this time, you could switch to a senior dog formula that has been designed to meet the nutritional requirements of the older Blue Heeler, while giving him a decreased number of calories.

As your Blue Heeler ages, nutrition is very important. Proper nutrition is key to good overall health and is the first line of defense against the onset of disease and age-related conditions. When your Blue Heeler or Australian Cattle Dog hits his golden years, be sure to consult with your veterinarian, to make sure that you are giving your dog the optimal senior dog formula and the right amount of food, to keep him happy and healthy in his later years.

How Are Diet and Health Connected in Blue Heelers?

Blue Heelers are generally a healthy dog breed, but they are susceptible to some skeletal and muscular problems. Good nutrition will help strengthen the Blue Heeler's musculoskeletal system and reduce the chances of contracting a bone or muscle disorder. Conditions such as arthritis, hip dysplasia, elbow dysplasia, cruciate ligament tear, and patellar luxation are all exacerbated by obesity, weak bones, and poor muscle tone. Some of these conditions are genetic, so you cannot completely stop them with nutrition, but nutrition plays an important role in the dog's overall health and fitness.

Though it requires a bit more thought, good nutrition will pay off for your Blue Heeler.

Is Dry Dog Food or Canned Dog Food Better, For My Blue Heeler?

Blue Heeler dog food comes in a few different types, primarily wet, canned dog food, and dry kibbles. Which type is best for your Blue Heeler? That is not a simple question to answer. Each type has its benefits and drawbacks, and it really comes down to personal preference.

Blue Heeler dry dog food, or kibbles, as it is called, is preferred by some because it is easier to store, easier to measure, and less smelly than canned dog food. Kibbles don't spoil as fast as canned. They are easy to take with you on the go. On top of that, dry dog food is typically less costly than canned food.

Canned dog food, also called wet or moist dog food, may be easier for an older Blue Heeler to eat, especially if he has some dental or digestive issues. For picky eaters, canned food may be more appealing. It has a stronger odor, so it may entice a finicky Blue Heeler dog to give it a try. There are some drawbacks with wet dog food. However, it is typically more expensive than dry dog food, and there is more waste. Canned Blue Heeler dog food cannot remain in the dog bowl for very long, because it spoils quickly. Lastly, canned food is harder to measure. To provide the correct amount of food for your Blue Heeler, you may find that you have to split a can among two feeding times. You will need to refrigerate the opened can to keep it fresh, and some pet owners complain that the strong smell of the canned dog food taints the human food in the fridge.

Some Blue Heeler dog foods are better than others, and this goes for both kibbles and canned food. It is possible to find top-quality products in both types of dog food, but it is also possible to purchase poor-quality dog food with very little nutritional value. Be sure to thoroughly read the dog food labels and discuss your options with your veterinarian before you settle on a brand and product for your Blue Heeler.

What Should I Know About Raw Diets?

One of the newest trends in the dog food industry is the raw food diet. Basically, the idea behind the raw food diet is to offer your Blue Heeler a variety of foods that closely mimics the types of food that he would eat in the wild. Just like canned and dry dog food, there are some positive benefits to a raw dog food diet, and some concerns.

People who advocate for a raw dog food diet state that the processed foods, chemicals, and preservatives often found in commercial dog food products are harmful to the animals. They believe that a clean diet is best, and quite frankly, they aren't wrong. Whether you opt for a raw diet or a more traditional one, you should strive to serve food that is as free of unnatural chemicals as possible. In general, the fresher the food and the closer it is to its raw, natural state, the more nutrients, vitamins, and minerals it contains.

Called the BARF diet, which stands for Biologically Appropriate Raw Food, this nutrition option has a following of supporters who believe in the benefits of this approach. Dogs fed a BARF diet are said to have a healthier, thicker coat, with less shedding, better digestion, fresh-smelling breath, stronger immune system, and reduced chances of skin allergies.

The United States Food and Drug Administration, however, does not recommend the raw diet for dogs, primarily because of the risk of contamination that raw meat carries. Raw meat, including raw meat purchased at a butcher shop, has a higher amount of bacteria. This is acceptable for human consumption because it will be cooked, but if you plan to give the raw meat to your Blue Heeler, you will be running the risk of too much bacteria for your dog. Some pet stores now sell raw meat for dog owners who want to follow the raw food diet. Since these products are meant for raw consumption, they are produced in such a way that the bacterial count is less. If you decide to try the BARF diet for your Blue Heeler, it is important that you follow good hygiene and food handling procedures, to reduce the amount of bacteria and contamination in the meat.

Your Blue Heeler will also enjoy playing with his food at times!

What Do I Need to Know About Making Homemade Dog Food, For My Blue Heeler?

Some Blue Heeler owners decide to make their own dog food for their animals because it gives them the peace of mind to know exactly what is going into their pet's food. You can make sure that your Blue Heeler dog food is as fresh as possible and made with top quality ingredients when you make homemade dog food. However, the process is expensive, and time-consuming. Before you commit to making your Blue Heeler's food from scratch, you should discuss your plans with your veterinarian. He or she can help you decide on the best recipe to follow, to produce a homemade dog food that satisfies the nutritional requirements of the Blue Heeler dog.

The drawbacks of making your own homemade dog food are the cost, mess, and time commitment. Buying all of the ingredients is costly. Fresh meat and vegetables spoil quickly, so you may find that you are running to the store several times a week. Cutting up raw meat is messy and unpleasant. The entire process of making homemade dog food takes time. You will need to combine exact amounts of animal protein and fat, with carbohydrates, such as whole grains, rice, and fresh vegetables. The recipes need to be followed exactly, and you should not substitute any of the ingredients. Any deviation from the recipe, may decrease the nutrient value within it.

Lastly, you should ask yourself why you want to make homemade dog food for your Blue Heeler and if you really have the time and money to do it properly. If you are not totally committed to making homemade dog food, you are probably better off purchasing commercial dog food. Dog food manufacturers have veterinarians, biologists, animal nutritionists, and chemists on staff, that constantly work to develop dog food formulas. These are educated and experienced scientists who have made a career out of perfecting dog food. Sometimes it is best to trust the experts.

What Dog Treats Can I Give My Blue Heeler?

We give our dogs treats for various reasons: as an incentive to learning tricks, a reward for good behavior, or just because they are so darn cute. But you should acquaint yourself with the different brands of dog treats that are on the market so that you select the best Blue Heeler dog treats for your dog.

Like commercial dog food, dog treats come in a wide range of forms and different levels of quality. You can find some really good treats that are healthy and packed with nutrients, and you can find some that have very little nutritional value…and all points in between.

A current philosophy with dog treats is to use them to supply additional vitamins and minerals. The goal is to use treats to improve the Blue Heeler's overall health and fitness, not to detract from it. In this regard, dog treats have morphed into vitamins or supplements for Blue Heelers. That is, if you find the right ones.

Moderation is the key when it comes to giving treats to your Blue Heeler. If the dog gets too many tasty treats, he may refuse to eat his normal dog food. Treats are not designed to meet all the nutritional needs of your Blue Heeler, so a diet of treats will lead to nutrition-related health problems. Treats should be given sparingly, so your dog is not filling up on empty calories.

What Foods are Dangerous to Blue Heelers?

Blue Heelers, or Australian Cattle Dogs, should not be fed a diet of table scraps. Human foods can be toxic to dogs, and some are downright deadly. For example, grapes and raisins contain substances that can cause acute kidney failure in dogs. Onions have a component known as thiosulphate, that is highly toxic to dogs. Macadamia nuts are one of the most poisonous human foods a dog can eat. Macadamia nuts can cause a spike in body temperature, vomiting, and the inability to walk. All parts of the avocado contain a substance called Persin, that causes diarrhea and vomiting in Blue Heelers and other dog breeds. The methylxanthines found in chocolate can damage to the dog's metabolic process. A sweetener called Xylitol that is found in sugar-free gums and candy can be deadly to dogs.

In addition, Blue Heelers and other dog breeds should never be given bones to chew on. These can splinter and lodge in the animal's throat. Fried and fatty foods are difficult for a Blue Heeler to digest, and can cause vomiting, diarrhea, and lethargy.

In general, it is the responsibility of the dog owner to make sure that the Blue Heeler is eating a diet that will supply him with the best minerals and nutrients to keep him in tip-top shape. Understanding the role of nutrition in the health of Blue Heelers will give you the information you need to make informed decisions about your dog's diet.

CHAPTER 9

Blue Heeler Training: How Is It Done?

Blue Heelers, or Australian Cattle Dogs, have two important traits that make them easy to train… they are highly intelligent, and eager to please. With this combination, the Blue Heeler is an exceptional work dog that is trainable, especially if he has a strong and experienced handler. Blue Heeler training should begin at an early age and continue through adulthood. This chapter is devoted to Blue Heeler training and provides tips and suggestions for training Blue Heeler puppies and Blue Heeler adult dogs.

What Should I Know About Blue Heeler Training?

Blue Heelers are confident, dominant dogs. If they feel that their master is weak or unsure, they will take over. You will find that you have become the second-in-command, and the Blue Heeler is boss. For this reason, you should only get a Blue Heeler if you are experienced with training dogs, and can provide a firm and consistent training regime. Even a veteran dog handler would benefit from getting a good Blue Heeler training book and talking to other Blue Heeler owners for tips.

How To House Train Your Blue Heeler Puppy

One of the first and most important lessons for your Blue Heeler puppy is house training or housebreaking. Potty training your Blue Heeler puppy is as much about training you, as it is about training your dog. You need to be observant for signs that your little Blue Heeler pup is about to poo or pee, and when he shows these signs, you need to whisk him outside or to his puppy pad. These signs can include sniffing around, whining, wandering toward the door, and hiding in corners or under furniture. Pretty soon, he will get the message that he is supposed to do his business outside.

Blue Heelers thrive on routine. First thing in the morning, about a half hour after mealtime, and after naps, are typically the times when your puppy will feel the need to go. Start your puppy on an established routine as early as you can, and you can train him to relieve himself at the times you determine.

In general, Blue Heelers are quick learners so, with patience and persistence, you puppy should be housebroken in no time.

Training for Basic Obedience...Sit, Stay, and Heel

The three basic dog commands of sit, stay, and heel, or come, are not only vital to get your dog to obey you, but are ways to keep your Blue Heeler safe as well. Once your Blue Heeler puppy knows how to sit on command, you can have him sit to keep him safe from fast-moving cars, or other potential dangers. You can teach your dog to sit, by giving the verbal command "sit," as you gently push down the dog's rump. Be sure to reward your pup with praise and a tasty treat to reinforce the lesson.

To avoid repeating the sit command constantly, you next need to teach your Blue Heeler puppy to stay and come, also called "heel." You can do this by first getting your puppy to sit. Then take a few steps away from the dog. If he follows you, take him back to his original position, and have him sit again. You will have to practice this again and again until your Blue Heeler figures out that you want him to stay. At first, only walk a few steps away, and have him stay for just a few moments. Work up to walking further away, and having the dog stay for longer periods of time. Be sure to reward his success with treats and praise. Be sure to keep the lessons fairly short, but to practice frequently. In no time at all, your smart Blue Heeler will understand when you want him to sit and stay, and when you want him to come to you.

Training your Blue Heeler will take a bit of patience, but will pay off in a more rewarding relationship.

From puppyhood, you should get your Blue Heeler used to walking on a leash. First, you need to get your pup used to the feel of the leash and build a familiarity with the leash. Once the leash ceases to be a novelty for the puppy, he will not be as interested in pulling and yanking on it. Always take care that you don't pull on the leash too hard, yourself. If the Blue Heeler refuses to walk, just stop and wait for the dog, while keeping forward pressure, on the leash and collar. The Blue Heeler will get used to the sensation of the collar and leash in due time and will soon be proudly walking on the leash when he goes for his walks.

How to Train to Correct Bad Behavior

Your Blue Heeler is a smart dog so he will learn his lessons quickly, but it also means he could pick up bad behavioral habits too. If you are not careful, this behavior can evolve into a permanent habit. When your Blue Heeler is naughty and digs, barks, chews, begs or jumps up on people, you need to immediately address the bad behavior in a firm and stern way. Consistency is the key. If you are not consistent with your discipline, you will be sending mixed signals to your dog.

First, you need to establish yourself as the pack leader. Once your Blue Heeler accepts you as the head of the pack, he will begin to respect your role as the boss, and his role as the second-in-command. It is important that your Blue Heeler learn his proper place, so you don't find yourself in a power struggle with your dog. He will accept your discipline and learn the rules more quickly, after he comes to respect you as the leader.

Some specific bad behavior requires specific training to correct. As a puppy, your Blue Heeler will probably chew on some of your belongings. This is a natural act. In fact, it relieves the discomfort from teething. You can train your puppy to stop chewing with a verbal command, like stop or drop, so you can let your puppy know when he has hold of something he shouldn't have.

Having your Blue Heeler under control will be a lot more satisfying than the alternative.

Fortunately, Blue Heelers aren't a very vocal breed. They occasionally do bark, but they are not known to be excessive barkers. If he does bark at strangers or knocks on the door, calmly quiet your dog, and then use positive reinforcement to reward his good behavior. This will help to train your Blue Heeler to know when and where it is an appropriate time to bark. The same goes for jumping up on people, digging, and other bad habits.

The sooner your address the negative behavior and help the Blue Heeler learn to moderate it, the quicker he will learn what his parameters are.

How Do I Train My Blue Heeler to do Tricks?

Blue Heelers like to be challenged to learn new things, so they are happy to work on new tricks with you. Once he masters sit, stay, and come, you can move on to learn more complicated tricks, like how to shake or give high-fives, roll over, or fetch. Blue Heelers need to keep their active minds busy, and learning new skills is one of the best ways to do this.

CHAPTER 10

How Do I Keep My Blue Heeler Healthy?

Your Blue Heeler dog depends on you to keep them healthy and in the best physical condition possible. In addition to regular veterinarian visits, you should brush up on the common ailments that can afflict the Blue Heeler breed. If you know the warning signs and symptoms of these diseases, you may be able to catch them early before your dog has lasting issues. Staying on top of the health of your Blue Heeler is part of the commitment you undertake when you welcome a dog into your life.

How Should I Find a Veterinarian For My Blue Heeler Puppy?

One of the first things you should be as a new dog owner is to establish a rapport with a nearby veterinarian. Ask friends and family members who they use for their dog's vet, or ask the breeder you purchase your puppy from who they recommend for a vet. Your new Blue Heeler puppy should visit the veterinarian for a check-up fairly soon after you bring him home. This will be your first step in giving your new Blue Heeler puppy a lifetime of health.

The Vet will be your trusted partner in keeping your Blue Heeler happy and healthy.

What Should I Know About Vaccines For My Blue Heeler Puppy?

Vaccines are your first line of defense against common diseases and help to set a foundation for good health for your Blue Heeler. Not will your Blue Heeler be protected from illness, but the vaccines will also ensure that the other dogs your dog comes in contact with will not contract a disease from your pup.

The vaccine schedule below is the one that is recommended by veterinarians for optimal health. Vaccinating your Blue Heeler is also required by law in most areas, and you will need to show proof of vaccination when applying for a dog license. There may be additional vaccines required for your dog depending on the city, state, or region you live in. It is always a good idea to check with your trusted veterinarian, and follow his or her advice regarding the vaccines requirements for your dog.

Puppy Age	Recommended Vaccines	Optional Vaccines
6-8 weeks	Distemper, measles, parainfluenza	Bordetella
10-12 weeks	DHPP (vaccines for distemper, adenovirus [hepatitis], parainfluenza, and parvovirus)	Coronavirus, Leptospirosis, Bordetella, Lyme disease
12-24 weeks	Rabies (not required in the UK)	None
14-16 weeks	DHPP	Coronavirus, Lyme disease, Leptospirosis
12-16 months	Rabies (not required in the UK), DHPP	Coronavirus, Lyme disease, Leptospirosis
Every 1-2 years	DHPP	Coronavirus, Lyme disease, Leptospirosis
Every 1-3 years	Rabies (not required in the UK)	None

Will My Blue Heeler Puppy Have His First Vaccines While At The Breeders?

The Blue Heeler breeder you purchase your puppy from will probably make sure that the puppies have their first round of vaccines, before they go to their new homes. In fact, you should be cautious of a breeder that doesn't vaccinate their puppies when they are still in their possession. This is a common cost-cutting move on the part of puppy mills or unscrupulous breeders. The puppies should have their first round of vaccines between the age of six and eight weeks and a reputable breeder will make sure that this happens on schedule. In fact, a good breeder will provide documentation of the dog's first vaccines that you can take to your veterinarian. This will be added to your Blue Heeler's health record at the veterinarian.

Veterinarians and animal scientists have determined that puppies do not need to be vaccinated until they are between six and eight weeks old. That is because puppies retain some of their mother's antibodies and immunities from birth, until they are a month and a half to two months old, so they are protected at the beginning of their lives. Vaccines in dogs work the same way that they do in humans. A weakened or dead strain of the disease is introduced into the dog's body. The pup's natural immune system will respond to the disease by building up defenses. That way, if the dog's body faces a threat from that particular disease again in the future, it has the appropriate antibodies all ready and waiting to fight it off.

*Maintaining proper vaccinations will mean you can have your
Blue Heeler in nature, without much worry.*

At regular intervals: at seven weeks, ten weeks, thirteen weeks, and sixteen weeks, your puppy will need to see the veterinarian for additional vaccinations to protect against such diseases as distemper, parvovirus, parainfluenza, and leptospirosis.

In addition to these inoculations, you may be required to have your Blue Heeler puppy vaccinated against kennel cough, known as internasal bordetella. This vaccine is typically administered between the ages of eight and sixteen weeks for puppies that are in close contact with other dogs, such as animals that frequent a doggie daycare, doggie play park, dog shows, or are housed overnight at kennels. You will find that most of these places require proof of the internasal bordetella vaccine.

When your Blue Heeler puppy is a bit older, between four and six months, he will need a rabies vaccine (unless in rabies-free places like the UK). He will need to have additional rabies inoculations every year. For dogs living in areas where rabies is more common your dog could also need a rabies booster shot halfway between the first rabies injection and the second-year rabies shot. Your veterinarian will be able to determine if this is necessary.

There are a few other optional vaccines that you may want to consider giving to your Blue Heeler puppy. One of these is the coronavirus vaccine. The coronavirus is usually not deadly to dogs, but in unhealthy dogs, coronavirus presents as a secondary infection, and can cause severe diarrhea and dehydration.

The second optional vaccine is the Lyme disease vaccine; spread through tick bites, Lyme disease is dangerous, but usually not deadly. A dog suffering from Lyme disease will experience fatigue, stiffness, and joint pain. The real problem with Lyme disease is that it flares back up from time to time over the course of the dog's life. For this reason, dog owners living in certain regions are advised to vaccinate their Blue Heeler dogs against Lyme disease. This is really the best way to protect your pet from the disease.

What Are Common Diseases Affecting Blue Heelers?

Hip Dysplasia in Blue Heelers

When the tip of the dog's femur doesn't fit properly into the hip joint socket, the dog is suffering from hip dysplasia. Hip dysplasia is a fairly common affliction among medium and large breed dogs. It can lead to pain and limited mobility, especially as the dog gets older. Genetics is one of the main causes of hip dysplasia in Blue Heelers. If the condition is present in one or both of a dog's parents, their offspring are at an increased risk of having hip dysplasia. There are additional factors that can contribute to the condition. Poor nutrition is one of them. Another is the environment. Some studies show that puppies that regularly climb stairs from birth to three months old may be at an increased risk of developing hip dysplasia later in life. Also, Blue Heelers that do not have adequate exercise space may develop hip dysplasia.

Routine care can keep your Blue Heeler healthy and smiling, and should never be skipped.

Progressive Retinal Atrophy in Blue Heelers

Blue Heelers are just one of the dog breeds that are prone to Progressive Retinal Atrophy, or PRA, a genetic condition affecting the eye. The retina is the part of the eye that captures incoming visual data and transmits it to the brain for decoding. For dogs suffering from PRA, the retina begins to degenerate between the ages of three and five years old. The Blue Heeler's eyesight gradually gets worse, until the animal is completely blind. There is no cure for Progressive Retinal Atrophy, but a simple DNA test will show if your dog carries the genetic marker for PRA.

Von Willebrand's Disease in Blue Heelers

Similar to hemophilia in people, Von Willebrand's Disease, commonly called vWD, in dogs is a blood disorder in which the blood does not properly clot, as it should. This is especially problematic if the Blue Heeler is injured or undergoes a surgical procedure. Because the dog's blood does not clot, he is prone to prolonged bleeding incidents that can be extremely dangerous. Fortunately, pet owners don't have to wait until their Blue Heeler is injured to find out if he suffers from vWD. A DNA test can be used to see if the dog may have vWD.

Cardiomyopathy in Blue Heelers

Cardiomyopathy is a heart condition in which affects the heart muscles. The heart becomes weaker as the walls of the heart become enlarged, and can no longer effectively pump blood. This heart condition impacts some dog breeds more than others and, fortunately, Blue Heelers are not on the high-risk list, but that doesn't mean they won't get the disease. If they do, your first indication that there is something wrong may come when the Blue Heeler acts lethargic and weak, with coughing and shortness of breath. As the disease progresses, he may have a distended abdomen, too.

Unfortunately, there is no cure for cardiomyopathy. There are, however, steps that can be taken to keep your dog's heart in good working order as long as possible. These include blood pressure medication and medicine to help reduce the fluid in his lungs.

Deafness in Blue Heelers

Genetic deafness in dog breeds is an odd thing. The gene that causes the hearing loss seems to be connected to the gene that is responsible for white or merle fur around the head. The deafness typically presents itself when the animal is still a puppy, and it can occur in one or both ears. Unfortunately, the hearing loss cannot be reversed, and it is often recommended that the animal be put down (but this is, of course, a personal choice). A deaf dog is often untrainable and may startle easily, which could cause him to snap and bite.

CHAPTER 11

What Do I Need to Know About Blue Heeler Grooming?

Blue Heelers have been called a "wash and wear" dog, meaning they don't require a lot of maintenance to keep them looking their best. But Blue Heelers or Australian Cattle Dogs are meant to be working dogs. They may spend the bulk of their days outside, running through tall, grassy fields or woods or streams. They will probably get dirtier than non-working dogs, which means they will require some cleaning on top of the normal grooming. In this chapter, we will look at the Blue Heeler grooming requirements.

You should get your Blue Heeler comfortable with grooming when he is still a small puppy. Train him to sit or stand still while he is being bathed or brushed, and to be calm when getting his nails trimmed. If you start regular grooming for your Blue Heeler as soon as he becomes a part of your family, he will learn how to behave during grooming time. But, if you don't condition him to be groomed, he may become distressed, agitated, or uncooperative, when you try to brush him or clip his nails. It will become more of a challenge for you, and a major source of trauma for him.

Good grooming starts with keeping your Blue Heeler clean, and a bit of basic maintenance.

Blue Heeler Grooming Tools

Before you can groom your dog, you need to have the right grooming tools and supplies on hand. In fact, it would be a good idea to buy these items ahead of time so that they are available to you when you need them.

There are several kinds of Blue Heeler dog brush. A bristled brush is your basic dog brush, made with tightly mounted, flexible bristles. The bristle brush is not only effective at removing dirt and debris from the Blue Heeler's coat but is a good way to help evenly distribute the natural oils that the animal secretes, to keep his coat shiny and healthy.

A slicker brush has short, metal bristles arranged on a square or rectangular pad with a handle. The slicker brush is designed to give the Blue Heeler's coat a smooth, glossy look after he is brushed with a bristle brush, but it is also good for untangling matted or snarled fur.

A rake-style dog brush looks just like the name implies, like a small rake. The type of Blue Heeler brush is useful when the animal is shedding because it gets in to the undercoat and helps you remove the excess fur. Blue Heeler shedding also happens as the puppy matures, loses his puppy fur, and gains his adult coat.

You will also need dog nail clippers so you can trim your Blue Heeler's toenails, and a pair of tick tweezers. When purchasing Blue Heeler nail clippers, look for a sturdy pair that has an opening big enough for your Blue Heeler's nails. The clippers should be sharp enough to cut the nail, and not crush it. A dedicated pair of tweezers that you can use to remove ticks from you Blue Heeler's skin is also a good grooming tool to have on hand. You never know when your hardworking Blue Heeler will bring in an unwelcomed guest, and you probably don't want to use your cosmetic tweezers for this job.

Lastly, you will need to have a good dog shampoo on hand. Blue Heeler dog shampoos should be pH balanced so that it is not too harsh on your dog's skin. Look for a shampoo formula that is strong enough to clean your Blue Heeler's fur, but gentle enough that it won't strip away the natural oils on the dog's coat. Never use human shampoo on your Blue Heeler. The pH balance is different in human shampoo and could harm the Blue Heeler's skin. If your Blue Heeler is a working dog that is out on the ranch or farm for a good part of the day, you may want to buy a good quality de-skunking shampoo to have on hand, if your Blue Heeler ever gets sprayed by a skunk. This way you can immediately bathe your sad and smelly Blue Heeler, instead of making him wait while you run to the pet store in search of de-skunking shampoo.

What Do I Need to Know About Blue Heeler Bathing?

In general, Blue Heelers like the water and don't mind taking a bath. If you get your Blue Heeler used to bath time as a puppy, he should learn to enjoy the bath without getting too squirmy, too combative, or too traumatized.

Whether you bathe your Blue Heeler in your bathtub or shower, in a kiddie wading pool, or a in a large tub, make sure to put a rubber, suction-cup bath mat down, so he doesn't slip and slide around. This will prevent him from getting injured, and you from getting soaked.

If you are worried about water splashing into your Blue Heeler's ears, which could lead to infections, you can place a cotton ball in each ear. But again, this is a practice you should start at an early age, so your Blue Heeler doesn't panic when you do it.

After you lather the shampoo into all parts of his fur, make sure that you thoroughly rinse it out. If shampoo is left on the dog's fur, it could collect dirt and look matted. There are some leave-in Blue Heeler conditioners on the market that will help your dog's coat look healthy and shiny. Look for one that contains mink oil, because this has been shown to add a sheen to the Blue Heeler's fur.

Well-groomed Blue Heelers show that you have a sense of pride and respect for your dog.

What Do I Need to Know About Blue Heeler Toenail Care?

Most of the time, Blue Heelers that are used as working dogs will keep their nails down naturally from running outside on abrasive rocks. But not always. If your Blue Heeler's toenails get too long, it becomes painful for him to walk and run and may lead to infections. Routine nail trimming should be part of your Blue Heeler grooming routine.

Nail trimming can be traumatizing for both you and the dog. To alleviate as much of the stress and anxiety as possible, get your dog used to the procedure when he is a young puppy. Then, he will know what to expect during nail trimming time, and how he should behave.

A pair of good quality dog nail clippers that are sharp enough to cut through the Blue Heeler's nails is essential. The trick with using these is not to trim the nail down too far. If you have more than one dog, or find that you are trimming your Blue Heeler's nails often, you may want to invest in a Dremel, an electric rotary tool, and specially designed dog nail sanding disks. This tool sands down the excess nail, and smoothens as it goes. Many dogs prefer the Dremel because it does not squeeze the toe nail, like conventional dog nail trimmers do.

What Do I Need to Know About Blue Heeler Dental Care?

Dental care for all breeds of dogs, including the Blue Heeler, is important to the overall health of the dog. Some studies have shown that, by the age of three years old, as many as 80% of dogs will show signs of dental or periodontal disease. You can prevent this by getting your Blue Heeler accustomed to teeth brushing from an early age.

When the Blue Heeler puppy is young, you can use a fingertip toothbrush, a soft-bristled doggie toothbrush that slips over your index finger, that allows you to clean inside your dog's mouth easily. As he gets bigger, you will want to graduate to a regular doggie toothbrush.

Purchase doggie toothpaste from your veterinarian or local pet store. Never use human toothpaste on your dog. Human toothpaste contains added fluoride that, even though it strengthens teeth, is also toxic. We humans know how to spit after we brush, so we really don't ingest much, or any, of the toothpaste. But your Blue Heeler will not understand that he needs to spit. Instead, he will consume the toothpaste. Specially formulated doggie toothpaste is non-toxic, and safe for Blue Heelers to eat.

What Do I Need to Know About Blue Heeler Ear Care?

Your Blue Heeler's ears are sensitive machines. Routine maintenance can keep them free of dirt and debris. There are several good Blue Heeler ear cleaning solutions that can be purchased at your local pet store. They come in a variety of formats, from wipes and rinses, to oils and drops. You should never insert anything too far into your Blue Heeler's ears. Instead, cleanse the area around the ear. If you are unsure of how to care for your Blue Heeler's ears, you should ask your veterinarian for a demonstration. He or she should be happy to show you the proper way to clean your dog's ears.

CHAPTER 12

Should I Show My Blue Heeler?

For more than one hundred years, dog enthusiasts have shown off their best dogs at dog shows. Not only is it an excellent way to see how your dog compares to other Blue Heelers, but it gives you an opportunity to meet other people who share your love of the Blue Heeler breed. If you are considering becoming involved in dog shows with your Blue Heeler, there are some important things to know ahead of time. In this chapter, we will discuss the things you need to know about showing your Blue Heeler dog.

Showing your Blue Heeler is challenging but really rewarding
if you have a love for the process.

How Are Blue Heelers Classified By Kennel Clubs?

The first thing to know if you plan to show your Blue Heeler
is that you probably won't see Blue Heelers listed among the
recognized breeds. That's because the breed is listed as the
Australian Cattle Dog, its alternative name, in most national
kennel clubs. In both the American Kennel Club and the
Canadian Kennel Club, the Australian Cattle Dog is a member
of the herding group of dogs. The Australian Cattle Dog is
included in the pastoral group of the Kennel Club of the UK.
In the Australian National Kennel Club, the Blue Heeler is
also listed as the Australian Cattle Dog, and is categorized as a
working dog.

Can Any Blue Heeler Be Shown at a Dog Show?

The way that animals are judged in a dog show is by comparing them, not to each other, but to the breed standards for that breed. The dogs need to be as close to the breed standards, as possible. The goal of dog shows is to show off breeding animals. That means, the Blue Heelers cannot be altered in any way. Dogs that have been spayed or neutered do not qualify for entrance into dog shows. Therefore, if you intend to have your Blue Heeler compete in dog shows, you cannot have him or her fixed as a puppy.

How Do I Select a Good Blue Heeler Puppy to Compete in Dog Shows?

If your goal is to enter your Blue Heeler in dog shows, you will need to do more research before you purchase a Blue Heeler puppy. Look for a Blue Heeler breeder who has a reputation for producing winning dogs. You may want to attend a few local or regional dog shows, and try to connect with award-winning breeders. They may also be able to give you tips about raising a champion Blue Heeler, from nutrition and socializing, to training and grooming.

What are the Acceptable Coat Colors for Australian Cattle Dogs?

Both Blue Heelers and Red Heelers are shown under the Australian Cattle Dog category in national kennel club shows. Acceptable coat colors are blue speckled, blue mottled, red speckled, and red mottled.

Are Blue Heelers Good For Dog Sports Competitions and Agility Contests?

There are several kinds of dog events and dog sports competitions, including agility, obedience, and diving. Blue Heelers are highly-intelligent dogs that are obedient, trainable, and want to please their owners. In addition, Blue Heelers are elite athletes. They are agile, fast, and have a tremendous amount of stamina. All of this makes Blue Heelers ideal for dog agility and sporting competitions.

CHAPTER 13

What Do I Need to Know About Working Blue Heelers?

Blue Heelers, or Australian Cattle Dogs, were developed to be working dogs. They are especially adept at working on sheep and cattle ranches. Their innate herding instinct means that the Blue Heelers know that they need to gather the livestock under his watch. But the Blue Heeler's work ethic and abilities – including his endurance, his intelligences, and his agility – make this breed a good worker in other areas, not just herding.

Working comes naturally and joyfully to the Blue Heeler!

Blue Heelers As Herding Dogs

Since they were developed to herd cattle and sheep, it is only natural that Blue Heelers are commonly found working on ranches. The breed was developed in Australia, so Blue Heelers are adapted to the heat and rugged terrain of the Australian outback. The alternate name of this breed, the Australian Cattle Dog, indicates the purpose of the dog. The energy level of the Blue Heelers is extremely high; these dogs go hard all day long. Blue Heelers are smart dogs. In fact, professor Stanley Coren lists the Blue Heeler in the number ten spot, on his list of the smartest dog breeds in his book, *The Intelligence of Dogs*. Their high intelligence level, as well as their fierce loyalty, means that Blue Heelers working on cattle ranches can work independently with little guidance.

Blue Heelers As Therapy Dogs, Service Dogs, and Emotional Support Dogs

Although many people lump service dogs, therapy dogs, and emotional support dogs together, there is an important distinction between the three. Blue Heelers can be used for each one of these jobs. Therapy dogs work in places like rehab centers, hospitals, schools, and counseling centers. The job of a therapy dog is to provide comfort and security to people who are ill, injured, or emotionally distraught. Therapy dogs work with many people, but emotional support dogs are assigned to work with one person exclusively. Studies have shown that petting a dog reduces blood pressure, stimulates the release of endorphins, and relieves anxiety and stress. Service dogs, on the other hand, are trained to do specific jobs for their owner, who is not able to do these tasks on their own, due to illness or disability.

Blue Heelers are friendly dogs that want to please their humans. They are friendly to strangers, too, which is a good quality to have for therapy dogs. Blue Heelers have other qualities that make them ideal candidates to be therapy dogs, emotional support dogs, and service dogs…they are intelligent, calm, patient, adaptable to different situations, and genuinely enjoy interactions with humans.

Blue Heelers excel in many areas and have many talents which can be leveraged for human benefit.

Blue Heeler Search and Rescue Dogs

Blue Heelers were specifically bred to have a lot of endurance and stamina. That trait is ideal for tracking dogs, or search and rescue dogs. They are able to stay on the trail, with few breaks. Blue Heelers learn quickly, and can be trained to do follow a scent and locate lost or injured people. Blue Heelers are well-equipped to work in rocky, over-grown regions, making them ideal search and rescue dogs.

Blue Heeler Drug-Sniffing Dogs

More and more police departments, airport security agencies, and homeland security departments are employing Blue Heelers, or Australian Cattle Dogs, as drug sniffing dogs. All dog breeds have excellent senses of smell, but it is the other traits that Blue Heelers bring to the table that make them useful as drug sniffing dogs. Their work-ethic, loyalty, and attention to detail move Blue Heelers to the top of the pack of other drug- sniffing dogs.

CHAPTER 14

What Do I Need to Know About Blue Heeler Breeding, Pregnancy, and Birth?

Once you have gotten to know the Blue Heeler breed and have experienced owning a few of the dogs yourself, you may be tempted to want to breed your Blue Heelers. Before you jump into an endeavor like this, you need to do a lot of research. Your duty is to be a good steward of the Blue Heeler breed, so you will want to approach your dog breeding in the most responsible way possible, so that you maintain the integrity of the breed. The last thing you want to do is to become a backyard breeder or puppy mill, yourself. In this chapter, we will provide an overview of the breeding process, as well as Blue Heeler pregnancy and birth, but this in no means is intended to be an encouragement for inexperienced breeders to attempt to breed Blue Heelers. This task is best left to the professionals, and those willing to learn what it takes.

Blue Heeler Breeding is a serious responsibility, as the breed itself is at stake.

How Do I Find a Mate For My Blue Heeler?

If you have done your homework and have some experience in dog breeding and how to breed your Blue Heeler, the first thing that you need to do is to find a mate. Of course, you want the mate to be a top-quality healthy dog, that has come from the best breeding stock. Check with your veterinarian to see if he or she can put you in contact with a Blue Heeler breeder in your area. Perhaps they have a male Blue Heeler that they would be willing to mate with your female Blue Heeler.

You can also locate a mate by talking to other Blue Heeler owners at kennel clubs and dog shows. Often, word of mouth is the best advertising. You may meet someone at a dog show in your region who knows someone else with a female Blue Heeler they want to mate with male Blue Heeler. Making the rounds where Blue Heeler owners congregate and making your needs known, is a great way to make contacts.

Lastly, you could check with sheep or cattle farmers in your area. If they use Blue Heelers as working dogs on their farms, they probably know Blue Heeler breeders in your area. They may be willing to put you in touch with a dog owner looking to breed his Blue Heeler.

What is the Blue Heeler Heat Cycle?

All dogs are individuals, so your female Blue Heeler will come into her first heat cycle on her own timeframe. On average, most dogs have their first cycle when they are about six months old, but some start earlier and some later. Some take as long as one to one and a half years of age. After that first heat cycle, you can expect your female Blue Heeler to stick to a pretty consistent cycle, coming into heat about every six months.

You can look for signs that your Blue Heeler is starting her cycle. She may have swollen nipples that are tender to the touch…she will shy away from you when you try to feel them. This is a result of hormone changes she is experiencing. She may also be moody and grumpy instead of her usual playful, cheerful self. You could see a bloody discharge from her, too, but most female dogs keep themselves clean, so the blood is not always apparent.

When a female Blue Heeler is in heat, she will give off hormones that attract males to her. You may notice an unfamiliar dog or two lurking in your yard. Female dogs make sure the males can catch her scent, by engaging in "flagging." She will hold her tail high in the air and wiggle it from side to side to spread her scent, and let nearby dogs know that she is ready to mate. During this time, you should keep your Blue Heeler sequestered. If she is allowed to run unsupervised around your yard or farm, she may breed with a doggie Casanova that stops by for a brief encounter.

What Should I Know About the Blue Heeler Mating Process?

When your female Blue Heeler is ready to mate, there really isn't much you can do to help. But the key is to know when she is ready. If you put two dogs together before the female is ready to mate, you may end up with a dog fight on your hands. That's because the female will be giving off hormones and scents that arouse and excite the male dog, but the female is thwarting his advances. This will cause agitation, and the male Blue Heeler may act out aggressively.

To know when your female Blue Heeler is ready to mate, you can ask your veterinarian to check her. This is the most effective way, but not the most convenient. It may require multiple trips to the veterinarian's office, which is costly and time consuming. You could try the less-reliable "flag test." Scratch the female's rump at the base of her tail. She will instinctively lift her tail and wave it from side to side like a flag if she is in the fertile stage and ready to mate. This is a good indicator that you can put her together with the male Blue Heeler.

Watch for mating activity when you put the male and female together. Ideally, you should allow them to mate several times, just to make sure that she gets pregnant. Professional breeders will put the two animals together every other day, for the duration of the female's heat cycle so the two can mate often. You will be able to tell when the female Blue Heeler is no longer fertile, because she refuses to mate anymore. When you observe this, remove the male Blue Heeler and discontinue the mating.

What Should I Know About Blue Heeler Pregnancy?

Although you will probably be anxious to find out if your female Blue Heeler is expecting, you won't know for sure for about a month. After a month has passed, you should see a noticeable weight gain on your Blue Heeler mother-to-be, and her nipples will be swollen and protruding. If you are still unsure or if you want to rule out a false pregnancy, you can schedule a veterinarian visit. You veterinarian will be able to determine if you Blue Heeler is, indeed, pregnant. He or she may even perform an ultrasound, so you will know how many puppies she is carrying.

The average gestational period for Blue Heelers is around 63 days. Of course, this can vary by a few days. Also, if your female Blue Heeler spent several days with her mate, you don't know exactly which day she got pregnant. All this means that there will be a window of time, in which she may deliver. Throughout those 63 or so days, you should do everything you can to make sure your expectant mother is eating a proper diet, with an increased amount of protein, fat, and calories. She should also be getting plenty of exercise, and staying active. She may be a bit touchy and standoffish during her pregnancy, but she still needs your love and support.

All of this is about to pay off with a new little visitor, or 10!

How Do I Help to Prepare My Blue Heeler to Give Birth?

As the estimated due date draws near, prepare a spot for her to deliver her puppies. You could turn a box or crate into a birthing suite for your Blue Heeler mother-to-be, by lining it with newspaper or puppy pads then placing clean, soft blankets or towels on top. The box or crate should be put in a quiet spot in your home, that is away from any high-traffic areas. A spare bedroom or walk-in closet works well. Once the crate is in place, introduce the area to your Blue Heeler. Encourage her to go inside and check it out. Hopefully, she will understand that this is a safe, secure place in which she can deliver her puppies.

Of course, this doesn't mean that she will use the birthing box, when the time comes. Don't be surprised to find a litter of puppies on your bed or behind your couch or on a pile of dirty clothes in the laundry room! If you see signs that she may be close to giving birth, you can try to coax her into the box, but don't force her to go there. If she doesn't feel secure there, you will only be causing her excess stress during a time when she needs to relax and focus on the impending birth.

What Should I Know About Blue Heeler Labor and Delivery?

The first thing you should know about Blue Heeler labor and delivery is to know when the process is starting. There are signs to look for to determine if your mother-to-be is in labor. She may pace the floor, pant excessively, and appear anxious. She may paw at her pile of blankets in an attempt to arrange them, in a more suitable way. She may sneak quietly off somewhere by herself, preferring to be alone for the birth. She may even lick herself more to clean up discharge that signals the onset of labor.

Once the birthing process starts, the best thing you can do is to stay out of the way. There is really nothing you can do to help her, and if you are too close to her, you may cause her to feel anxious or stressed. You may feel helpless watching her give birth but remember that giving birth is completely natural, and dogs rarely require assistance from humans. It is best to try to interfere as little as possible, and let nature take its course.

Instruct all family members, especially those who stay to watch the birth, to remain calm and quiet. In fact, you will probably have to remind young children of this several times. It is tempting to want to cheer and shout as a new puppy emerges. This will only startle the new mother and interrupt her focus on the birthing process. Instead, encourage children to speak slowly in hushed voices to keep the Blue Heeler calm.

During the birthing process, your Blue Heeler will most likely deliver her pups about twenty minutes apart. But remember that this is just an average. She could appear to be done, then deliver another puppy two or more hours later. The average litter size for Blue Heelers is five puppies, but that, too, is just an average. Your Blue Heeler could have just two or three puppies, or as many as eight. With an unknown litter size, it is hard to know when the process is done. Just be patient.

After each puppy is born in the birth process, the mother-to-be will chew off the umbilical cord and embryonic sac. Sometimes, however, another puppy is born before she is finished cleaning up the first puppy. This is totally normal. Your Blue Heeler mother will return to the task as soon as she can. You will only cause her anxiety and stress, if you try to give her a hand and clean off the puppy yourself. She is in a heightened emotional state and won't take too kindly to you taking one of her new pups away. You also do not need to step in and help, if you see a puppy being born tail first. In humans, that is a breech birth that could lead to complications, but in a dog, it is perfectly normal. Just allow the Blue Heeler mother to do her thing, and you will most likely see a happy ending.

Once you are sure that all of the puppies have made their arrival and labor and delivery for your Blue Heeler mother is over, offer the new mother some water. After all, she just completed a tremendously taxing accomplishment, and is probably thirsty. She may even want a bit of food. If your Blue Heeler mother acts like she needs to go outside to relieve herself, allow her to. But you may want to usher the family out of the room first, so that the new mother feels comfortable enough to leave her newborns for a few minutes.

In the next day or so, try to replace the soiled and bloody bedding with clean blankets or towels, but only do it if it will cause minimal disruption to the new mother and her newborn Blue Heelers.

Blue Heeler puppies can be a lot of fun and aren't that hard to care for.

How Do I Care For the Newborn Blue Heeler Puppies?

For the first few weeks, there isn't much for you to do in caring for the newborn Blue Heeler puppies. Their mother will be doing most of the work. The babies will sleep most of the time, and feed when they are awake. They will be helpless until their eyes are fully open. The best thing you can do is to allow the mother to take care of them. After a few weeks, the puppies will be more mobile, and you will see their individual personalities begin to emerge.

As soon as the puppies are born, you should work to find them good homes. It is not practical to keep all of the puppies, as cute as they may be. Talk to dog clubs in your area and to your veterinarian to get the word out that you have Blue Heeler puppies available. As a responsible breeder, you will need to have each one of the puppies examined by your veterinarian and given their first round of puppy immunizations. Start them on a diet of top-quality puppy food. Then, when the puppies reach about eight weeks old, they will be ready to go to their forever homes.

CHAPTER 15

Are Miniature Blue Heelers Legitimate?

One of the current fads or trends in the dog industry is to create miniature versions of popular dogs, generally to give owners the illusion of perpetual puppyhood. While some dog breeds have several legitimate size variations, such as miniatures or toys, the Blue Heeler is not one of them. There is no true miniature Blue Heeler dog breed.

Reputable Blue Heeler breeders are focused on preserving the breed and producing pups that meet the breed standard. No respectable Blue Heeler breeder will tamper with the dog's genetics in order to produce a smaller version of the dog. To them, it is unethical and goes against their commitment to being good stewards of the Blue Heeler breed.

If you see an advertisement for Mini Blue Heelers, you should be skeptical. Most likely, the miniature Blue Heeler puppies they have for sale are not purebred Blue Heelers, but are mixed with a much smaller dog breed in hopes of producing an animal that looks like a diminutive form of the Blue Heeler. While these puppies may be cute and cuddly, they may have health issues from the unscrupulous breeding practices.

When you are in the market for a dog, you owe it to all of the different dog breeds to help maintain the integrity of the breed. If you want a smaller, toy-sized dog, there are plenty of toy breeds to choose from. Supporting the unethical breeding practices of greedy backyard breeders who only hope to profit from selling tiny dogs is wrong, and would be doing a disservice to the Blue Heeler dog breed.

CHAPTER 16

What Are Common Blue Heeler Mixes?

Blue Heelers have so many admirable qualities that it is only natural that Blue Heeler owners may want to breed their animals with other dog breeds. One of the current trends today is so-called designer dogs, a term for a mixed breed dog. Unlike traditional mixed breeding, designer dog breeding is more controlled and done by reputable breeders to ensure consistent results, in both physical characteristics and personality. Throughout this chapter, we will look at some of the more popular Blue Heeler mixes, all with clever portmanteau names and terrific characteristics that enhance the already-wonderful features of the Blue Heeler.

Aussimo

An Australian Cattle Dog, or Blue Heeler, that has been crossed with an American Eskimo Dog is commonly called an Aussimo. A medium sized hybrid dog, the Aussimo is a friendly and active dog that is both intelligent and inquisitive. From the American Eskimo Dog, Aussimos inherit a wariness toward strangers, but, like the Australian Cattle Dog, they are loyal and affectionate to their owners. Aussimos usually retain the coloring of the Australian Cattle Dog, either the blue speckled or mottled coats or red speckled or mottled coats, but their fur is longer, softer, and fluffier than purebred Blue Heelers.

Labraheelers

When it comes to Blue Heeler designer mixes, the Labraheeler is one of the newest creations. The combination of the Blue Heeler with a Labrador Retriever creates a slender, medium-sized dog that can resemble either one, or both, of the parents' breeds. Labraheelers are terrific family dogs; they are gentle, sweet, loyal, and patient, even with children. Both Labs and Blue Heelers are high-energy dogs, so Labraheelers are as well. They thrive in busy, active families and need a large, fenced yard and plenty of opportunities for exercise.

Pit Heeler

An American Pitbull Terrier and Blue Heeler hybrid is called a Pit Heeler. Although they can be sweet and loving, Pit Heelers can be stubborn and domineering dogs. Therefore they are best when owned by an experienced dog owner, one who can take control and let the Pit Heeler know who the boss is. Pit Heelers often have thick, dense fur, so they prefer to live in cooler climates.

Cattle Shepherd

The hybrid of a Blue Heeler, and a German Shepherd produces a confident, hard-working, and protective dog, called the Cattle Shepherd. Cattle Shepherds tend to be slightly larger than purebred Blue Heelers and, because the parent dogs both excel at herding sheep and cattle, the Cattle Shepherds are excellent working dogs for ranches and farms. This designer dog makes a good watchdog, and can be trusted to watch over livestock. Cattle

Shepherds can exhibit dominating and intimidating behavior, however, so they do better with a strong, experienced owner who can lay down the law.

Border Heeler

When a Border Collie is bred with a Blue Heeler, the resulting pup is called a Border Heeler. Both Border Collies and Blue Heelers are among the smartest dog breeds so you can expect a Border Heeler to be extremely intelligent and a quick learner. Border Heelers need to keep both their minds and bodies active. If they get too bored or don't get enough exercise, they may act out by engaging in destructive behavior, including excessive barking, digging, and chewing on random objects. Border Heelers thrive when they are mentally and physically challenged.

Ausky

A hybrid of an Australian Cattle Dog, or Blue Heeler, and a Siberian Husky, the Ausky is a dog that is as smart as he is beautiful. Who can resist the piercing blue eyes of a Husky? Auskies are active dogs, that are often too smart for their own good. They require early socializing and a firm owner to prevent them from becoming stubborn, defiant, and destructive. But with a strong owner and consistent discipline, the Ausky is playful, friendly, and outgoing. Some Auskies inherit the Blue Heeler's instinct to herd and nip, so this might not be the best dog to have around young children.

Box Heeler

When one crosses a Boxer with a Blue Heeler, a Box Heeler is the outcome. Box Heelers are another relatively new hybrid, or designer dog breed. They tend to be larger and stockier than purebred Blue Heelers, with more muscle mass. Box Heelers tend to be curious, playful, and energetic. The breed, in general, enjoys few genetic health issues. But like Blue Heelers, Box Heelers are happier when they are working. Having a job to do keeps them physically active, and keeps their mind alert

CHAPTER 17

How Do I Care for My Aging Blue Heeler?

T he average life expectancy for a Blue Heeler is between 13 and 15 years. Around the age of ten, your Blue Heeler will enter into his senior years. This is a time of change for your Blue Heeler, when he will go through a number of changes to his disposition, this physical body, and his mental capacity, that are all part of the natural aging process. In this chapter, we will discuss the changes your Blue Heeler will experience as he ages, so that you can understand what your dog is going through, and how you can ease his transition through his golden years.

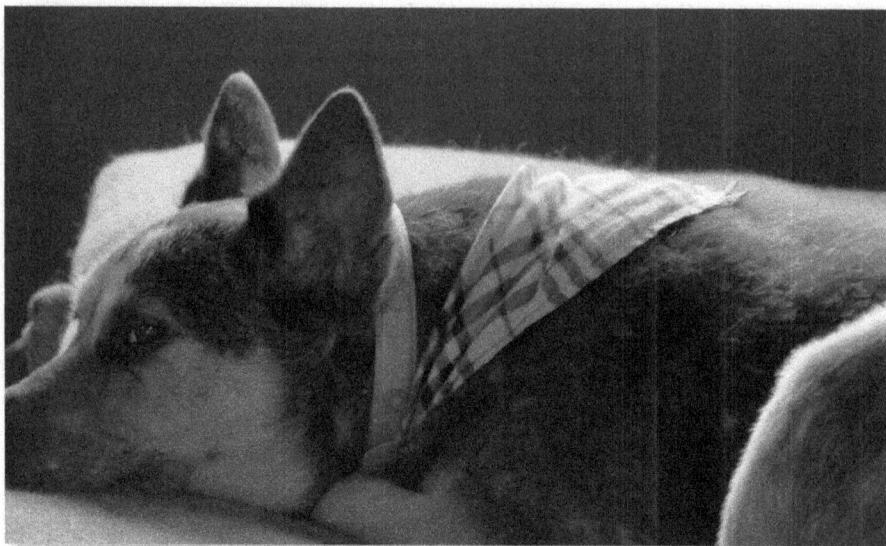

Blue Heeler golden years can be quite rewarding for both you and your dog, with a little extra care.

What Changes in Diet and Nutrition Will My Blue Heeler Experience?

Nutrition is important at every stage of your dog's life, including his senior years. But older dogs often experience changes to their digestion and metabolism, that mean their current diet might not work for them anymore. As your Blue Heeler ages, you should continue to discuss his diet and nutritional needs with your veterinarian and make adjustments in your dog's food, based on the recommendations of your veterinarian.

The first change your veterinarian will most likely suggest would be switching your Blue Heeler to a senior formula dog food. Senior formula dog foods have fewer calories than adult formula dog food, but still contain the vitamins and nutrients that your Blue Heeler needs. Most commercial dog food brands offer their products in several different formulas, including a puppy formula, adult formula, weight loss formula, and a senior formula, so you may be able to stick with the brand you have always used, and just switch to a different formula.

If you continue to feed your older dog the same dog food formula and the same quantity as your Blue Heeler ages, you may notice that he is packing on the weight. That's probably because most dogs are less active as they age. Gaining excess weight, however, can have a negative impact on your Blue Heeler's overall health. It could cause joint pain and make certain medical conditions worse. In fact, obesity in dogs will reduce their life expectancy. To keep your Blue Heeler feeling good, looking good, and in your life longer, you need to make sure he maintains a healthy weight.

However, some Blue Heelers have trouble keeping the weight on as they get older. This might be because they simply aren't eating their food. Changes in their digestive system could be the culprit. Or it could be that the problem is with their teeth. If your older Blue Heeler has lost some teeth due to old age, chewing might be hard for him. If this is the case, you should consider switching your Blue Heeler to a canned dog food that will be easier for him to chew.

What Changes Will Occur in My Blue Heelers Drinking Habits and Bowel and Bladder Functions?

Some medical conditions that are common in older dogs, such as decreased kidney function and diabetes, may increase your Blue Heeler's thirst. You may notice that he is drinking a lot more water, or that his water bowl is often empty. A larger bowl or an on-demand waterer may help.

A result of increased thirst is that your Blue Heeler will need more potty breaks. It can be frustrating to repeatedly have to take your Blue Heeler out to relieve himself. Please realize that dogs lose their ability to hold their bladder for long periods of time as they grow older.

Along with frequent potty breaks, you may notice that your older dog is having accidents in the house. This, again, is common as the dog ages. If your Blue Heeler, that has always been so good about his house training, suddenly starts urinating or having bowel movements in the house, don't punish your dog for this, no matter how upset you are. Your dog is not being defiant or being vindictive toward you. He simply can't hold it. In fact, your Blue Heeler will probably feel shame over the deed. It is unfair to punish him for something he cannot help.

Of course, you can't have your Blue Heeler ruining your house either. The solution is to let your Blue Heeler outside more frequently and to put down puppy pads when you are away from home for a longer period of time. You could even gate your Blue Heeler in an area of the house that is easier to clean, like a room with tile or linoleum flooring. Lastly, you could consider hiring a professional dog walker or dog sitter, to stop by every day to let your Blue Heeler outside to relieve himself.

There are many reasons for bladder or bowel control issues in older dogs. If your Blue Heeler is having issues with bowel or bladder accidents, you should schedule a visit with your veterinarian, to rule out a disease or other non-age-related problems.

Aging Blue Heelers require a bit more patience, as they do sometimes have issues which they cannot help.

What Do I Need to Know About Joint Pain and Stiffness in Blue Heelers?

Your Blue Heeler has probably always been such an active dog, so it may break your heart to see him moving slowly and painfully, because of joint issues. Joint pain and stiffness are very common in dogs, as they age. Bear in mind that your Blue Heeler may not be vocal about the pain he is in. But there will be signs to indicate that he is stiff and sore. He may seem reluctant to climb stairs, or jump up into the tailgate of your truck. He may be slower to get up from a sitting position. These are all signs that he may be experiencing stiffness and joint pain.

Schedule a visit with your veterinarian to have your Blue Heeler examined and to discuss his joint pain. Your veterinarian will look for the cause of the stiffness and joint pain so he or she can best determine how to treat it. It may be arthritis, or it could be hip dysplasia. Prescription medication may help to control the pain, by reducing inflammation.

One thing to remember about Blue Heelers is that this is a dog breed that loves to please his owner, and enjoys long work hours. Even as his body is telling him to slow down, your Blue Heeler's mind it is telling him to keep up his old work habits. This all means that it will be easy for your Blue Heeler to over-exert himself. As he ages, you should gradually cut back on the physical activity and the work that your Blue Heeler does, and also offer plenty of breaks. Your stubborn and determined Blue Heeler will probably still be thinking "go! go! go!" so it is up to you to get his to start slowing down. He has, after all, earned his retirement.

What Do I Need to Know About Vision and Hearing Problems in Blue Heelers?

As often happens in humans, Blue Heelers sometimes experience a drastic decline in their vision or hearing, when they hit their senior years. If this happens, it could really change your dog's quality of life. There are some things that you can do to help.

First, of course, is to schedule an appointment with your veterinarian, so you Blue Heeler can get a thorough examination. Your dog's veterinarian may be able to determine the cause of the hearing or vision loss and offer suggestions for stopping the progression.

When hearing declines, your dog may startle more easily. He simply cannot hear when a person or animal approaches. You should advise all members of your family to approach the dog slowly, without sudden movements. Sometimes, an older dog that is startled may react by snapping or nipping. Even with hearing loss, dogs can feel vibrations. Stomping loudly as you come near the dog, clapping, or knocking on things, might produce enough vibrations so that your older Blue Heeler knows you are near.

Blue Heelers are a breed that loves to please their owner. When his hearing begins to fail, he may not be able to hear your commands, or at least, not hear them clearly enough to understand. During this time, you can rely more on hand signals, to give your commands.

If your Blue Heeler's vision fails, he will probably still be able to move around familiar areas, like your house and yard. Don't rearrange the furniture, however, or it will totally confuse your aging Blue Heeler. In fact, the more you can keep things the same, the happier he will be.

A Blue Heeler that is going blind may stick by your side more than normal. Although it might be annoying to have your dog constantly underfoot, remember that he is probably frightened and confused by his eyesight loss and is comforted by being close to you. Give him the love and reassurance he needs to navigate his golden years with as little stress and anxiety as possible.

Blue Heelers continue to feel loyalty to you even as they slow down, in older age.

What Do I Need to Know About Memory Loss and Confusion in Blue Heelers?

Just as humans sometimes get forgetful in their old age, dogs can also experience memory loss, disorientation, and confusion. You may notice that your Blue Heeler seems to forget a person that he knows well. He may also sleep or relieve himself in places he never did before. It is tough and scary to see your old friend experience memory loss…and even scarier for him. You can help your Blue Heeler by keeping his environment consistent, and offering him plenty of love and comfort. It is a difficult thing to do, but you should also try to forgive him for accidents or misdeeds. There is a really good chance that he is not being defiant. He's just confused, and doesn't remember what is acceptable behavior, and what is not.

What Do I Need to Know About Changing Personality and Disposition in Blue Heelers?

As your Blue Heeler enters his golden years, you may notice that his personality has changed. Many of the changes in his disposition and behavior can be traced back to physical pain, hearing or vision loss, and confusion. In addition, your Blue Heeler may just act like a grumpy old man! He may be less patient with other pets, less tolerant of noise and chaos, and less energetic. This is common. The best thing that you can do is to make his life as comfortable as possible. Train your other pets to leave him alone. Ask your children to refrain from roughhousing with your older Blue Heeler. Stick to a good nutrition plan, with vitamin supplements, and just be encouraging yet calm.

Above all, remember that your Blue Heeler has spent his life with you. He has worked for you, and has been a loyal companion. He has earned himself a cushy retirement.

CHAPTER 18

Conclusion To The Blue Heeler

The Blue Heeler, or the Australian Cattle Dog, is a special dog. A hybrid of domestic herding dogs and Australia's wild dingoes, the Blue Heeler is one of the smartest breeds. He is well-suited to do the work that he was developed to do, and is equally at home on a sprawling cattle ranch as he is in a suburban family home. For a dog breed that was developed from wild dogs, it may come as a surprise to many to learn that the Blue Heeler loves human companionship. Blue Heelers are truly man's best friend. Their loyalty, companionship, and eagerness to please, makes them a sought-after working dog and family pet, yet the breed is still a best-kept secret.

The intelligence and confidence of the Blue Heeler means that they require an owner and handler that is strong, consistent, and commanding. This is probably not the breed for the first-time dog owner. If the Blue Heeler senses weakness or hesitation in its owner, it will barge in and take control. The Blue Heeler needs an owner who can quickly and firmly establish himself as the dominant alpha, and show the Blue Heeler his place.

Once the pecking order has been established, however, the Blue Heeler will happily accept his position in the pack and work to please his owner.

Blue Heelers are one of the most rewarding breeds out there, and you will be in for a rewarding journey!

Blue Heelers were developed and bred for long, hot days on the cattle ranches of Australia. They are a high-energy breed that require a lot of physical and mental activity to keep stimulated, fit, and happy. Blue Heelers are ideal for farms and ranches or with busy, active families. Never content to be couch potatoes, Blue Heelers want to go, go, go.

As a fit and muscular, medium-sized dog, the Blue Heeler is not as susceptible to some of the health concerns that plague large breed dogs, including hip dysplasia and heart disease. With a proper diet, plenty of exercise, and lots of love and attention, the beautiful Blue Heeler will enjoy a happy life and will return the favor with years of loyalty and comradery. Thank you and enjoy your wonderful Blue Heeler journey, something you surely will cherish!

Your Trusted Blue Heeler Resource List

This bonus chapter offers you additional information that you may need to find a Blue Heeler breeder or a Blue Heeler rescue organization near you. While this is by no means a comprehensive list, it does provide you with the information you will need to locate the perfect Blue Heeler to join your family.

Thank you for reading this book and enjoy the experience!

Blue Heeler Breeders in the United States

- **Timber Kennels**
  https://www.timberkennels.com/
  Georgia
- **Hirehand Kennels**
  http://www.hiredhandkennel.com/index.html
  Georgia

- **Hardtack**
  http://www.hardtackacds.com/
  Texas
- **Sleepy Hallow Cattle Dogs**
  http://www.sleepyhollowcattledogs.com/
  North Carolina
- **Greenfield Puppies**
  https://www.greenfieldpuppies.com/blue-heeler-australian-cattle-dog-puppies-for-sale/
  Pennsylvania
- **Buffalo Creek Cattle Dogs**
  http://www.ksranchheelers.com/
  Wyoming
- **Mill Creek's Cattle Dogs**
  https://www.millcreekscattledogs.com/
  North Carolina
- **Blue Red Joe's Australian Cattle Dogs**
  http://www.blueredjoes.com/
  California

Blue Heeler Breeders in Canada

- **Blue Heelers of Western Canada**
  http://www.blueheeler.ca/
  Saskatchewan

- **Reddenblu Kennels**
  http://www.reddenblu.com/aboutus.html
  Ontario
- **Agassiz Registered Kennels**
  http://www.agassizcattledog.com/
  Ontario
- **Uretopia Australian Cattle Dogs**
  https://uretopiaacds.com/
  Ontario

Blue Heeler Breeders in the U.K.

- **Brydindo Australian Cattle Dogs**
  bryndingo@btinternet.com
  Ceredigion, Wales
- **Garregddu Australian Cattle Dogs**
  https://garregddu.wordpress.com/
  West Yorkshire, England

Blue Heeler Rescue Groups in the United States

- **Texas Cattle Dog Rescue**
  https://texascattledogrescue.com/
  Texas
- **Australian Cattle Dog Rescue Association**
  https://www.acdra.org/
  Multiple States

- **Arizona Cattle Dog Rescue**

  https://arizonacattledogrescue.org/

  Arizona

- **Australian Cattle Dog Rescue of Illinois**

  https://www.australiancattledogrescue.net/

  Illinois

Blue Heeler Rescue Groups in Canada

- **Australian Cattle Dog Rescue of Ontario**

  https://savearescue.org/orgsandrescues/listing/australian-cattle-dog-rescue-of-ontario

  Ontario

- **Canada Australian Cattle Dog Rescue**

  http://australiancattledog.rescueme.org/ca

  Ontario

- **AB Herding Dog Rescue**

  https://www.petfinder.com/member/ca/ab/didsbury/ab-herding-dog-rescue-ab65/

  Alberta

Blue Heeler Rescue Groups in the U.K.

- **Australian Cattle Dog Rescue**

  https://www.petfinder.com/member/ca/ab/didsbury/ab-herding-dog-rescue-ab65/

  Multiple locations

www.ingramcontent.com/pod-product-compliance
Lightning Source LLC
Chambersburg PA
CBHW072156090426
42740CB00012B/2290